The Game Changer:
A Collection Of Poetry

To Karen,

Keep up all the hard work,
a person that values work is
a great worker. A person that values
people is a great person. Never stop
being both,

Regards,

Peter Howe

The Game Changer: A Collection Of Poetry

Peter Howe

ISBN: 1516918495
ISBN 13: 9781516918492
Library of Congress Control Number: 2015913679
CreateSpace Independent Publishing Platform
North Charleston, South Carolina

Dedications

This book is dedicated to many different people, first is my mother and sister who I love so much and I know will always support me, my best friend Stephen, who has been my friend for 20 years and may as well be a brother, Stacey who suggested the idea for the poem "May they rest in peace?" My distant cousin Steven Reid, who is like the older brother I never had. Stacey's mother Fran, who I know will cheer me on. My friends at the Manor, the banquet hall I worked at and several times asked them to listen to some of the poems and they did. I also want to thank my friends Rob, Steve and Chris who are always encouraging and always welcome me with open arms. I would also like to dedicate this book to the people at Curb Signs and Ellis Studios who finally allowed me the opportunity to excel in the accounting field. I also wanted to thank Leigh-Ann who was my counsellor during a difficult time in my life. Finally, I would like to dedicate this book, to anyone who tries to think bigger and who wants humanity to move forward rather than backwards.

Introduction

An idea can change the world, for better or for worse, obviously I hope for the former. As you read through this book, I hope more than anything else that it will push people to think critically and really examine the variety of topics discussed. I hope that the person who reads this doesn't ever say "I agree with Peter because he said it" or some version of that. If more people thought for themselves and about more things, and more importantly always being willing to reconsider their own point of view, the world would be a better place.

Some people may be curious as to why there are 71 poems in this collection, some may think that I just ran out of ideas. The actual reason is that I expect this book to become available in 2015 and 2015-1944 is 71. If someone is wondering the significance of the year 1944, when you read the poem "Game-Changer", you will know exactly why I chose that number and why it means a lot to me.

1
Second Chance Day

October the 28th, a day that goes unmarked,
yet I cannot forget how we almost embarked,
On the path of destruction, that we dodged by a wire,
A billion lives, almost engulfed in fire,
Some reached for peace, as others pushed for conflict,
some looked for innocence, as others looked to convict,
The other side, because it's all their fault,
they thought if we strike first, we win the assault,
A billion would have died, in a single day,
yet all others would have died, in a more gruesome way,
Countless more, would wither from radiation,
what a price to pay, for being a nearby nation,
What about those farthest away,
what would they have faced in their next day,
Nuclear winter, filling the sky with ash,
when there is no food, what good is cash,
All of humanity, exploded, poisoned and starved,
what sort of legacy would those actions have carved,
I cringe at the thought, of so many suffering that fate,
to stand for the power of love, and in horror of the power of hate,
If this brings a tear to your eye, don't feel ashamed,
I too lament that humanity, can be so untamed,
Now that I told you what wasn't, a new look at what was,
the missiles lowered and the rhetoric calmed because,
Sanity was placed above vengeance, empathy over anger,
to not know if you will see tomorrow, what a cliff hanger,
Let us not forget that day in 1962,

a day that should mean so much to me and you,
When they heard there was peace, and they let out a sigh,
because they didn't see a mushroom cloud, but a beautiful blue sky,
We should learn from our mistakes, but also celebrate,
when our better side won, on that crucial date,
We have our second chance, let us not waste a word,
because if we lose this chance, we may not get a third.
Written on June 3, 2013.

2
The Pedestal

It's my turn on the pedestal, and it feels so strange,
I don't know if I belong, in the upper range,
When others get their turn, they revel in superiority,
soaking in the praise, of their fraternity or sorority,
But when I hear their praise, it feels like a lie,
do they have me confused, with some other guy,
It doesn't make sense, I know how great I'm not,
yet they think I'm remarkable, a brilliant mind well taught,
As I ponder what is happening, I look up at the heavens,
I see humanity's potential, where we don't need lucky 7s,
As I look back down, and see so many so low,
it reminds me that there is so little we know,
Finally I come back, and wait for the norm to resume,
when will we rise, I can't predict or presume,
As I step down, and finish using my free speech,
I ask if we all stood taller, how high could the pedestal reach?
Written on June 4, 2013.

3
The Experiment

We wonder where we came from, and wonder where we're going,
everyone is guessing, but there is no way of knowing,
Evolution explains a lot, but doesn't know the spark,
was it an accident, or a god that lit up the dark,
There's another theory, that makes many pause,
could aliens have been the initial cause,
Of life on earth, an oasis of diversity,
continuing to survive, despite all adversity,
But if aliens got it started, we should ask why,
what would be their motive, to come from the sky,
And seed a planet, to start life anew,
to start a chain of events, that they couldn't undo,
What if their focus, was to build a human being,
a creature that is capable of seeing,
Beyond oneself, beyond infinity,
to raise science out of divinity,
If they came back, what would be their finding,
a dark depressing place, or a light that is blinding,
They would see small areas, of brilliance and hope,
surrounded by mountains of despair, in which few can cope,
Their experiment would be failing, right in front of their eyes,
billions competing, for the wrong prize,
Power, control, domination and oppression,
millennia after millennia, it is humanity's obsession,

As they got back in their spaceship, filled with despair,
perhaps thinking, that we are a waste of air,
One may raise his hand, and say let's try again,
wait 1000 years and they will be washed away by the rain,
And they may return, and may be stunned where they stand,
if we have turned our planet, into the promised land.
Written on June 13, 2013.

4
The Coin

The Coin is a symbol, but what does it represent,
greed, materialism, a very cheap present,
It represents the outlook, that so many believe,
the perfect tool, that so many use to deceive,
How many sides does a coin have, we all know it is two,
how many sides in a conflict, we all know it is two,
You are with us or against us, an ancient battle cry,
that gets us tangled on the ground, unable to fly,
There is always an enemy, there is always a threat,
was this the inevitable result, of when different groups met,
The enemy of my enemy is my friend, isn't that right,
is a friend someone, who shares our use of might,
It's so interchangeable, insert group here,
we have to destroy, this other group we fear,
They are monsters, criminals, everything that is evil,
we are what's right, a concept so medieval,
There is no middle ground, in the two-sided mind,
if they don't pledge allegiance, the two-sided will find,
A way to convince them that the enemy, is a clear and present danger,
that you should fear them, especially if they're a stranger,
No one can be on the edge, no one can be impartial,
no one can referee, and no one can marshal,
Because the two-sided mind is closed, no one can tell them they're wrong,
if you are on my side you are right, it's where you belong,
The story is so old, we've heard it our whole lives,
angry prejudiced people, meeting in their hives,

Ready to sting like bees, ready to attack the other side,
life is not so simple, complexity will never subside,
The first step is to see the edge, and to realize there is grey,
if you can make it there, maybe you can see the other way,
No matter how many times you flip the coin, remember the edge,
a jagged place where many people, stand on a ledge,
Some conflicts are necessary, and many are absurd,
yet the unnecessary ones, will never be cured,
Life will never be so simple, there will never be a day,
you can't cut the world in half, you will always fail, there is always grey,
There is one thing, that a coin can never ever do,
and that is remove the other side, the one that disagrees with you,
It will always have to accept the other side, and the edge,
it is with this realization that I make a pledge,
I will not let anyone, make me see the world in only one way,
a healthy coin is balanced, and that is the way it should stay.

Written on June 22, 2013.

5
Other Me

Countless worlds, countless versions of earth,
all of them varying wildly in their worth,
So it stands to reason, there are world's almost the same,
another me would exist, with the same name,
What if he and I were the same, down to the genes,
wearing the same clothes, down to the jeans,
Making the same moves, having the same thoughts,
having the same beliefs, connecting the same dots,
It continues this way, until a failure hits us both,
a failure so great, that it breaks our old oath,
To not accept failure, success is the only choice,
the failure breaks us both down, and puts a crack in our voice,
I pulled myself back up, and continued toward my goals,
the other me feels destroyed, his pride full of holes,
As I begin to succeed again, my confidence returns,
the other's soul feels helpless, as his hope burns and burns,
He believes he was doomed for failure, sabotaged from the start,
he was a fool for thinking, he could ever be a part,
Of the happy people, who succeed and are fulfilled,
who succeed through effort, luck, and being well skilled,
So as I lost weight and put down my edible crutches,
he dove deeper and deeper into food, and away from human touches,
He pushes away his friends, he believes they will betray,
it's only a matter of time, there will be a backstabbing day,
He becomes alone and bitter, and over 300 pounds,
anyone speaking to him, feels out of bounds,
As his emptiness grows, along with his weight,
he has reached his breaking point, and named his date,

When he will end his own life, because his life is too rough,
his tombstone will say "after 25 years, I'd had enough"
He was two days away, from the pavement calling his name,
his 25th birthday, he will feel relief from the shame,
He was alone in his apartment, trying to keep himself busy,
when a blinding light emerged, disorienting, making him dizzy,
It was an angel, telling him "it can be a wonderful life"
"bullshit" he declared, "I will never have a wife,"
He went on "no one wants me, I am one of society's outcasts,
people pretend to love you, but it never ever lasts,"
The angel grabbed him by the wrist, and said "you're in for a surprise",
and pulled him through a vortex, that overwhelmed his eyes,
When they reached their destination, it looked just like home,
the one that he lived in, before he went alone to roam,
And they saw the moment of his failure, seven years before,
and saw unlike him, I didn't stay on the floor,
As the angel showed him my life, that I did have some fun,
all that he had missed, and all I had done,
It was hard for him to believe, that he had been wrong all these years,
his life wouldn't have been perfect, but not held back by his fears,
One thing remained a mystery, he asked "what sets us apart?"
the angel said "no matter what he endured, he always had hope in his heart",
As he returned to his world, in a state of shock,
he spent the next two days, staring at the clock,
He went to the bridge, where the pavement calls his name,
could the rest of his life be different, or more of the same,
The pavement's call was loud, but another call could be heard,
a call of hope going through his mind, he wasn't just a nerd,

He could lose weight, he could find friends, there can be better times ahead,
soon the hope grew louder, louder than his desire to be dead,
He took a hard look at the pavement, and started to walk away,
the pavement's call grew silent, as he said "not today",
He knew it would never be easy, and it would be a hard road,
but he knew he could make it through, no matter how life flowed,
He walked towards the sunlight, with goals and ambition,
for the first time in years, hope gave him a mission,
A smile formed on his face, and he began to feel well,
there may not be a heaven, but his life would no longer be hell.
Written On June 25, 2013.

6
The Empty Ring

It's silent now, so quiet, so still,
nothing to look forward to, no countdown until,
The ring bell is sounded, the action begins,
not relenting, until one man wins,
The crowd on their feet, cheering these athletes,
performing the most incredible physical feats,
Some forget it's a sport, because they are telling a story,
yes they aren't competing, and they shouldn't be sorry,
It was once so popular, everyone knew their names,
images in my head, dreams in frames,
I am an old man now, a senior citizen with a tear,
showing my grandson, the sport I held so dear,
I tell him they packed arenas, thousands and thousands more,
to see it all so quiet, stuns me at my core,
He asked me what happened, who, where and when,
when did they fail, to inspire the dreams of men,
Did they give up on their heroes, because the villains won too much,
No the passionless writers, had lost their touch,
Politics overpowered logic, the egos running wild,
some were less mature, than an eight year old child,
Terrible management plagued some, as they lost millions of dollars,
but that didn't last long, they went under and abandoned their brawlers,
As companies collapsed, the top company stopped trying,
we thought it was a phase, we never thought they were dying,
A few bright phoenixes, rose from the ash,
we thought the industry was coming back, ready to have a bash,

But they began making the same mistakes, little was learned,
the fans were spit in the face, as they gave up and turned,
Entertainment exploding, the fans picked off one-by-one,
the less loyal will leave, when the show stops being fun,
The smaller companies died, as the fans mourned the loss,
the top company stopped caring entirely, they were the boss,
The writer's ignorance, made it a talk show,
boring the fans, who wanted matches to go,
The buy rates plummeted, and ratings went through the basement,
the sport of pro wrestling, was undergoing defacement,
Finally they gave up, the industry had died,
by this point the fan base, for independents had dried,
Now I stand in an empty ring, sad that I can't share my joy,
that captured my imagination, when I was a boy,
But I'm thankful my grandson's imagination, still flies like a wing,
I'm just an old man with memories, in an empty ring.
Written on June 25, 2013.

7
Invisible Prophecy

Que cera cera, whatever will be, will be,
some simply can't wait, show the future to me,
They will try to interpret tarot cards, just to get a clue,
some look into crystal balls, hoping for a clearer view,
Others look to the stars, thinking they're guided by a constellation,
waiting for the prophecy, waiting with salivation,
To think they can know the future, there's good things ahead,
they know what obstacles will come, they can put their fears to bed,
But how can we know the future, days or weeks in advance,
how many things in a day, happen purely by chance,
Is this simply a reach for power, a reach for unique status,
to reach for a place above, so they can look down from the stratus,
Some claim to be psychic, and make the boldest predictions of all,
inevitably with time, their credibility and predictions fall,
What do psychics think they're reading, an invisible prophecy,
the words of time itself, that only they can see,
Why does this idea persist, in the face of countless fails,
there's always a new crazy train, and some ready to ride the rails,
Why do they want all time to be written, by an unknown hand,
the hourglass controlling the direction, of every grain of sand,
Destiny and fate overrated, a concept scarier than we admit,
imagine every action decided for you, that you cannot ever quit,
The psychics prefer to talk about destiny, it's usually more upbeat,
you cannot fail, the unknown hand won't allow your defeat,
Perhaps the invisible prophecy, is for those afraid to fail,
perhaps it's for those afraid to tell a tale,

Of them falling short, of chance denying their goal,
but believing you have no free will, should take the greatest toll,
I don't believe an invisible prophecy, decides what will be,
I think it's up to us, you, them and me,
You can read your horoscopes, you can believe in psychics too,
but it might be because, you don't believe in you.
Written on June 26, 2013.

8
Revelation Indeed

So many, for so long, have been told here and there,
to go tell it on the mountain, over the hills and everywhere,
To spread the teachings of Jesus, to every corner of the earth,
that message is priceless, that it's immeasurable in worth,
Christify the earth, show everyone the way,
to some it's so important, who did you convert today,
There's another part of the message, the epic climax,
the epic battle of all time, countless bodies in stacks,
The number of the beast, beware the 666,
the ultimate battle that will fix,
Everything, the good will ascend, the evil will fall,
but something must be questioned about it all,
If the message spreads, and is accepted in every heart,
when the devil builds his army, who will take part,
If everyone is on god's side, the Anti-Christ would be alone,
no epic battle, could ever possibly be sown,
The world wouldn't need to end, a different future would be in store,
the world could keep spinning, for three billion years more,
What does all of this mean, let me tell you who are on the fences,
that this contradiction, has severe consequences,
First it guarantees, that there is always a foe,
some have to be the enemy, who, I don't know,
Not a good formula, for those who want peace,
it's not a good way, to have a long life to lease,
Beyond that some are looking, for the anti-christ,
this search has stolen time, a chronological heist,

Paranoia grips those, believing he's coming soon,
pointing fingers at leaders, who don't echo their tune,
Perhaps what's more troubling, than the inevitable scapegoat,
is that the mission was doomed to sink, like a hole in a boat,
Why would we be given a mission, that would never be completed,
why would the perfect message, not be the winner if it competed,
We are told to put our trust, to take the hand of the lord,
for him we will do anything, including swing the sword,
but why does he not have faith, isn't our redemption what it's all about,
if he loved us so much, why would he count billions out,
Perhaps god is cruel, setting us up to fight our brother,
that is one explanation, but there is another,
They are bad human ideas, that plant a seed of violence,
so many have stayed quiet, because safety was in silence,
If there is an epic battle, a war that makes the earth bleed,
it will resemble what they foretold, a revelation indeed.
Written on June 30, 2013.

9
A Hollow Halo

On the surface of surfaces, you can't tell who is evil or good,
some claim they can, but no one can and no one could,
You have to get to know them, and watch them close,
they might fool you for a while, evil loves to pose,
They have a fake smile, they fit in fully,
some are more transparent, and you can see the bully,
Some are cold and calculating, users of the truly kind,
these people are truly selfish, only they matter in their mind,
Some are liars and thieves, who will steal from their friends,
and they might do it again, after they've made amends,
Some will abandon their children, tossing them away with a thought,
never realizing they threw away, the love that they sought,
Never mind the rapists, murderers and the ones that didn't get caught,
how long can they keep up the act, that their soul didn't rot,
Let us not forget the celebrities, politicians and others in the spotlight,
so obsessed with their image, trying to come across just right,
Sure a few give to charities, and say the right phrases,
but you dig deep enough, and soon you see what's in their bases,
Shallow status climbers, looking for their own glory,
screw the truth, they can re-write their story,
Why are they all so despicable, the answers are numerous,
most are sad or disgusting, only a few are humorous,
Over their head is a halo, shining bright in the sun,
the rich ones wish, they could buy another one,

Peter Howe

But don't be thrown off, by the halo over one's head,
and listen carefully, to the words they have said,
Their actions speak louder than the halo, held up with wires,
they may not get hit with karma, and won't be in hell's fires,
But as long as you watch out, you may be able to dodge their con,
don't forget maybe, just maybe, you have real halo on.
Written on July 2, 2013.

10
Over There

I am fortunate to live where I do, one of the safest places,
a place where there is peace, among the different races,
Yet there is always something wrong, somewhere else, far away,
horror so unspeakable, but leaves me with much to say,
Some innocents are massacred, as many more have no water to drink,
some places ruled with an iron fist, and a few more on the brink,
It's always over there, somewhere away from us,
it seems so irrelevant, so meaningless and thus,
One death is a tragedy, a million is a statistic,
well a horrible statistic, I don't want to sound sadistic,
This stark contrast, makes many wonder,
how can we be civilized, and the others such a blunder,
Millions are sent, and hardly any progress is heard,
it's always getting worse, that is always the word,
Some have given up, it's just out of our control,
some want their government, to play a bigger role,
The racists point fingers and say they're savages,
thankfully few listen, we remember racism's ravages,
Some work tirelessly, dedicating their lives to the cause,
I applaud their character, but it gives me pause,
How tragically easy, for their work to be undone,
a militant gang, can burn down a village for fun,
People get sold, as if they're commodities,
in some parts of the world, these situations aren't oddities,

Other countries, are in a state of complete civil war,
if we had a tenth that much violence, our leaders would be shown the door,
With all of these facts, the case has been built,
by those who wish, to weigh us down with guilt,
With all the suffering, how can you sleep at night,
they will tell you until your wallet, is in their sight,
I wish I knew, what the solution was,
but I can reconcile reality, and sleep at night because,
I started with the numbers and an awakening hit me,
it was so intense, that this revelation bit me,
If you cried one second, for every person that died or is dying,
I have done the math, you would literally never stop crying,
So think about the problems, make yourself aware,
donate money, if you find a charity that does care,
But if you spend your whole life depressed, over what the world will do,
you never will have been fully alive, and someone will mourn twice as much
for you.
Written on July 3, 2013.

11
In your darkest hour

In your darkest hour, you don't remember the time on the clock,
the first five minutes, you are in a state of shock,
You cannot believe, what has occurred,
you cannot believe your senses, from what you've seen and heard,
The next 25 minutes, you are overtaken with despair,
feeling so weak, wondering why you should care,
About the rest of your life, it looks so damn bad,
you can't think clearly, there is no hope to be had,
The next 12 minutes are fear, wondering what's coming next,
when will the other shoe drop, and in what context,
Looking around the corner, absolutely paranoid,
wondering who's the next one with whom your heart will be toyed,
The next 12 minutes are anger, why does it have to be this way,
why did this happen, why me, why today,
Why does the world screw with me, there are others who are worse,
damn this world, that has laid me with this curse,
For five more minutes you are calmer, but frustrated,
add this to the list, of those times you've been aggravated,
The final minute, the most crucial of all,
to ask yourself, how can I once again stand tall,
You can look into the abyss, and resist the urge to blink,
your gears can turn, and you really start to think,
The clock chimes, and you have survived the hour,
and you begin to feel again, that you do have power,
Make no mistake, another dark hour will come,
for a few it comes rarely, it comes more often for some,

Remember you are human, you think second and feel first,
this fact is in our biology, our best quality and our worst,
In your darkest hour, you will feel like you crashed and burned,
but it is from this experience, that many have learned,
That the hour is very long, but your will must be longer,
and what doesn't destroy your resolve, makes you stronger.
Written on July 5, 2013.

12
The Search

We are all looking, for someone, some place or something,
our place in the world, whether as a peasant or king,
What am I good at, what do I have a passion for,
can I do this role for five years, and be willing to do more,
We are all searching for friends, a group in which we belong,
a place where we can be ourselves, that doesn't feel wrong,
And we all search for that soulmate, that makes us feel whole,
a person with whom we can tell, the darkest secrets of our soul,
We will spend endless hours in school, for a career,
believing it will be worth it, as we go to classes year after year,
Some find it fulfilling, many regret what they chose,
what is the right career, who really knows,
Sometimes your friendships fall through, maybe they're not who you thought,
it started small and became, a never-ending argument that you fought,
It's sad when you go through life, never finding your true love,
wishing and wishing, that they would fall into your arms from above,
To not have these are tragedies, a struggle I wish on no one,
to feel like you are missing out, on life's joys achievements and fun,
The greatest tragedy of all, even greater than these three,
a search many forget to do, until it happens they won't be free,
A search that can never, ever, go too far,
because the greatest tragedy of all, is not knowing who you are.
Written on July 10, 2013.

13
What's left to say

I can tell you how to be an artist, but I can't tell you how to get rich,
money should be secondary, not the point of your pitch,
You can paint, sculpt, act, or write as I'm doing now,
it's not complicated, I will tell you how,
It's about what do you have to say, and how do you want to say it,
it's about your expression of ideas, communication and wit,
There are two questions, every artist must ask,
first what if I'm terrible, at my chosen task,
Then you must face it head on, and keep trying as a hobby,
and keep in mind the people telling you that, might be very snobby,
The second one is harder to answer, "what is left to say?"
hasn't every idea been said, by someone in some way,
All those revolutionary ideas, haven't they already been taken,
won't my ideas be a copycat, abandoned and forsaken,
Give it time and thought, and you can develop ideas of your own,
observations and ideas, that some may not condone,
Because there are ideological battles, fighting to rule tomorrow,
if you don't raise your voice, your shyness may be your sorrow,
Add your voice to those calling for justice, where you find it lacking,
even if your ideas aren't original, sometimes it's important to show who
you're backing,
Maybe your ideas, aren't so controversial and large,
maybe they're simple and you're not trying to lead a charge,
But the point of art isn't about money, power, or fame,
you can often tell the difference, they're not all the same,

Those who only do it for money, follow the formulas set by another,
rather than plotting their own course, realizing their the father or mother,
Of this living thing, an idea from within their heart,
money is nice, but it shouldn't be the whole part,
So express your ideas, even if they're only seen by a few,
and if you make it big and famous, good for you,
Ask yourself as you finish your art, and you're wondering what to call it,
are you reaching for the heart, mind or wallet,
There are real artists out there, passion and tools in tow,
what is left to say, maybe you already know.
Written on July 10, 2013.

14
The blindfold replaced with blinkers

The metaphor is clear, the statue made with care,
justice is blind, so it will be balanced and fair,
It's a great ideal, everyone is equal under the law,
no one gets privilege, no one can rig the draw,
But it doesn't seem to work that way, the ideal remains out of reach,
for those who are minorities, the deal is not a sweet peach,
Given harsher punishment, because of the colour of their skin,
assumed to be criminals, by the ignorant and their kin,
It's sad when the statistics, are met with shrugged shoulders,
it can't be fixed, like going uphill pushing boulders,
Is it so much to ask, that a person is judged as an individual,
it hurts that person, but there is much more in the residual,
Bitterness, despair, faith lost in the powers to be,
why does this happen, do they really represent you and me,
The blindfold replaced with blinkers, not seeing the big picture,
law enforcement is too important, it's a permanent fixture,
But things have to change, leftover racism must fall,
or people will have no faith, in democracy at all,
Who will fight the wars, for a country that deserves to lose,
and if they are drafted, the nation has robbed their right to choose,
Patriotism is beautiful, if it's well founded,
and it's not lies and propaganda, that have sounded,
Some may ask why I care, I'm safe because I'm white,
I won't be racially profiled, when I drive home tonight,

I shouldn't have to be black, to know they're treated unfair,
I shouldn't have to be Jewish or Muslim, to welcome them anywhere,
I shouldn't have to be gay, to speak up for their rights,
I don't need to be a woman, to attack the misogyny in my sights,
I wish I could wake up more people, so they can start seeing,
all you should need to have empathy, is to be a human being.
Written on July 15, 2013.

15

White Dress

Every once in a while, we are invited to a wedding,
there's so much to think about, there is so much fretting,
Will we get them the right gift, will we get there on time,
if your gift isn't generous enough, it might be treated like a crime,
So you bought something off their list, and showed up with time to spare,
you have found a place to sit, and love is in the air,
Everyone gets into place, and music hits a familiar beat,
everyone looks behind them, and rises to their feet,
The bride comes out, in her beautiful white dress,
was it expensive, I'm sure we all can guess,
We are usually caught up in the moment, reveling in the romance,
but here is the question to ask, when you have a chance,
Why is it always white, why is it always that way,
why can't she wear a different colour, isn't this her day,
This has gone unexamined, decade after decade,
this is just the tradition, we don't remember why it was made,
White represents purity, never been with another man,
the woman shouldn't be with another, but the man can,
It's a sad double standard, leftover from old times,
when men owned women, and marital rapes weren't crimes,
The only way he could be sure, that the children were his own,
was to make sure she was a virgin, and control her to the bone,
We don't live in those times, thankfully we're evolving,
but it's a leftover attitude, causing problems in need of solving,
We all know the double standard, we've heard it from society's layers,
women who sleep around are sluts, men by contrast are players,

A woman's choice should be hers, not decided by prudes,
who flinch at any sexuality, even tamer than nudes,
If two people decide, they want to spend their lives together,
it should be their decision, how their marriage will survive the weather,
Marriage can be beautiful, at its best the definition of love,
at worst it's a walk through hell, waiting for the shove,
So don't rush into marriage, wait until you're sure,
you don't have to marry someone, who is "pure",
When it's your turn to get married, put your best effort in,
many ideas will pass, but keep this one in,
They are who they are, love them or let them fly like a dove,
remember to be equals, control is not love,
Let her wear any dress, whether it's white, red, or blue,
all that should matter is, that she's coming down the aisle to you.
Written on July 16, 2013.

16
Lines

So many threats, so much to worry about,
terrorism, causing explosions to ring out,
People trying to censor, expression of all sorts,
believing that the media, should be taken to the courts,
And climate change causing chaos, across the globe,
we've seen the effects in front of our eyes, no need for a probe,
These are all used, as calls to actions,
believing that these threats, will break the world in fractions,
Terrorism causes deaths, and fear for many more,
with new anti-terrorism laws, threatening constitutions at their core,
It is hard to know, how much media affects the mind,
how much or how little, are there other factors that bind,
Climate change, the biggest threat of all,
seems to be the doomsday clock, for humanity's fall,
We are still measuring the effects, some are in denial,
they think everything is fine, the planet's just adjusting the dial,
As the threats grow, the floods more severe,
people will become, covered in fear,
What will be the next super-storm, that wipes out a city,
destroying thousands of lives, without remorse or pity,
What will the people, be prepared to do,
to stop the disasters, desperation, building and new,
Will they throw away their rights, to do damage control,
as they fall into tyranny, deeper and deeper in the hole,
It will be for the greater good, or so they will say,
sacrifice for society, or future generations will pay,

Climate change may finally stop, several generations from now,
it will be the status quo, being ordered when, where and how,
Freedom thrown away, a discarded luxury,
that was sacrificed to prevent humanity's bury,
I am not naïve, these threats are not a fable,
but before all of this happens, or is even on the table,
If humanity is saved, at the expense of choice,
we should ask why can't we solve this, with our own voice,
It's noble that we want, future generations to live on the earth,
but if they are born and live as slaves, what is survival worth?
Written on July 20, 2013.

17
The most primitive of all

The greatest inventions, among the best is science,
looking for facts, not for mass compliance,
Sometimes the new facts, fly in the face of our myth,
this new information, so controversial, who to side with,
Some choose ignorance, believing in a divine plan,
and refuse to accept, the origin of man,
Utter ridiculous dogma, reasons truly absurd,
things so stupid, I can't believe what I've heard,
I'm not an animal, I'm above all of that,
god made humans special, I'm nothing like the cat,
We rule the planet, the bible says so,
I believe in the bible, that's better than what you know,
Why don't monkeys still turn into humans, see you're wrong,
billions of years, the earth ain't been around that long,
It goes on and on, the denial of reality,
exponential evidence of evolution, in its totality,
It's disgusting how many people, cannot accept the fact,
our ancestors were primitive apes, common ancestors to be exact,
What will it take, for the delusions to be set aside,
will the internet, break bad parenting and turn the tide,
There's an element of arrogance that prevails,
when you think you know everything, and refuse to accept your fails,
When you think you are divine, so myopic in your view,
that you think the universe was made for you,
You can distance yourself from chimps, with every ignorant call,
but choosing ignorance because it's easier, makes you the most primitive of all.
Written on October 12, 2013.

18
King of the Graveyard

We all know the story, when we were children we were told,
the story passed down, from generations of old,

Of a king, wise and brave, and a noble leader as well,
going on adventures, there are so many he could tell,
It's good to be the king, yes I'm sure it was,
to reign for a lifetime, long live the king was the buzz,
Complete job security, you are set for life,
with plenty of riches and women, not just your wife,
It seems bright and beautiful, but the nostalgia goggles are on,
there is a reason, I am glad that this time is gone,
The king is a nice title, people like to be the king,
But a different name and the same description, tells us something,
Dictator, Despot, Authoritarian, Fascist, Feurher,
The good vibes are all gone, king sounds purer,
But what is the difference, is there any at all,
is it just a myth sanitizing the past, with tales that are tall,
The king ordered to invade, the nation next door,
no matter how much wealth he had, he always wanted more,
The serfs at the bottom, were trapped below,
by the glass ceiling, guarded by swords, that all indeed know,
Any who dared to speak out, disappeared without a trace,
so hail to the king, remember your happy face,
Call it whatever you want, but the horror is there,
lurking behind a benign word, are massacres everywhere,
No matter what you call the monster, who left the nation scarred,
I hope we never again hail, the King of the Graveyard.
Written on February 10, 2014.

19

Pride Parade

Every June, there are annual celebrations
an event that stands out, among other nations,
Where they come out of the closet, and onto the street,
showing their true colours, in the sun and summer heat,
What is this event, is it just a party at its core,
or is it something bigger, is it something more,
It was half an hour in, when I saw the essence of the parade,
the reason why it exists, the reason why it was made,
It is defiance personified, it is what many have waited for their whole lives,
a chance to stand tall, to revel in loud music, the dancing and jives,
Putting their middle finger in the air, this is who I am and scream it loud,
I will not be hidden away, and forced to fit with the crowd,
I will not be a piece of clay, moulded to other's desires,
this is the day, where my passion burns brighter than fires,
The middle finger is to the puritanical, still around,
still stuck in the past, believing their ideas are profound,
A person wanting to live, in the world of Leave it to Beaver,
this parade spits in the face, of the worldview of that believer,
Thinking gay people are a few sinners, here they are by the truckload,
they are out in the open, there is no hidden code,
It used to be illegal, but the police are there in support,
being gay is no longer a reason, to be sent to court,
That isn't going to change, here comes a political party float,
showing whose side they're on, too bad the conservatives won't join the boat,
The religious are supposed to condemn this, and tell them they are going to hell,
but here come the floats, representing the religious as well,

The puritanical hate sexuality, the sight of it offends them,
well here comes the naked people, their society is rotting from the stem,
The polyamorous come, saying monogamy isn't for all,
the traditional idea of relationships, is undergoing a fall,
People smoking marijuana in the crowd, everyone's having a great time,
smiles a mile wide, people enjoying their prime,
All those traditional chains, holding people in their place,
the individuality forbidden society, had an assigned face,
But now people are questioning, and breaking away from the past,
leaving the puritanical jailers, mouths wide open, aghast,
Society won't explode, because people live a different way,
Not only can people be different, but parents can be gay,
Society doesn't have to be trapped, the roles arbitrarily assigned,
with rules and laws, only a bigot would have designed,
We are entering a new age, a sample shown every June,
where people can be themselves, and others welcome a different tune,
Now the biggest question of all, why do we need this parade,
if society is going to change, isn't the path already made,
Progress isn't constant, it always must be pushed ahead,
because those who man a blockade, will build walls made of lead,
So we must power through, and cast off the chains of conformity,
and the puritans will see, the better society's middle finger, in its enormity.
Written on February 17, 2014.

20

Memorial

We say they're no longer with us, passed on, passed away,
common euphemisms, used by many today,
A funeral is prepared, friends and family attend,
emotional wounds are clear, we hope in time they mend,
But is that truly it, is that truly all,

some want it more positive, a life celebration they call,
I have asked myself the question, what do I want for my turn,
for those that didn't know me, what do I want them to learn,
I have pondered this, the few times the subject appears,
time and time again, I don't know is between my ears,
One day when I least expected it, I saw what I searched for,
something that touched me, deep down in my core,
A video put together, for a friend who committed suicide,
showing the highlights, of their friendship's beautiful ride,
Beautiful smiles and laughs, to the tune of somewhere over the rainbow,
you saw his passion, he wanted to entertain and he did so,
But the part that meant the most, was his serious one,
a message from the heart, that gave me a stun,
he said you're not stupid, never tell yourself that you are,
what you have in your head is what makes you unique and who you are,
"You'll go out and do some wonderful things" as he continued through,
"and if no one else tells you this, I care about you"
A tragic case that such a loving person, isn't here on this date,
that he felt so overwhelmed, and couldn't carry life's weight,

But what I can take away, is not just the video's end,
but what his friends did, for their fallen friend,
Archiving his ideas and actions, so others can have them,
and allow them to have the entire message, letting them hear the entire gem,
Paying tribute is telling others, how great one was,
but showing it instead of saying it, is greater than testimony does,
I hope when my time comes, my wisdom is worth internet streaming,
I hope by then I truly am wise, and can help the young one's dreaming.
Written on February 25, 2014.

21

Iron Pyrite

It seems too good to be true, for riches it can be sold,
but it's a trick, hopes raised for nothing, fool's gold,
A quick glance fools most, it must be seen by an expert,
the revelation crushes you, into so much hurt,
Why don't I have the real thing, what bad luck,
it frustrates you how much the situation does suck,
The worst thing of all, is there are people like this,
people who you think, will lead you to bliss,
But it's an illusion, people who put on a show,
you just can't tell, it's all you know,
So don't feel too bad, if they fool you for a while,
it's only an expert, that can see through a smile,
Just watch them closely, time will bring their true selves to light,
and eventually you'll see who is gold, and who is fool's gold, Iron Pyrite.
Written on February 26, 2014.

22
Scrooge Returned

We all know the figure, Humbug he would say,
no compassion and maximum work, for minimal pay,
Not caring if their employees, could keep a roof over their head,
rather than helping the poor, he'd rather they be dead,
A money lender squeezing interest, squeezing blood from a stone,
not caring about the homeless, out in the cold, chilled to the bone,
But we've heard this somewhere else, we've heard this story before,
somewhere besides, Charles Dicken's famous lore,
Now I remember, it's reported in the news,
economic trends, where more and more people lose,
How did this happen, don't we have a minimum wage,
wasn't everyone told not to be greedy, from the youngest age,
The unions got workers, paid better and better,
until the day came, when they were told by a letter,
Your job is going somewhere, far, far away,
nothing could have made, those factory jobs stay,
For those who are left, no bargaining power remains,
as frustration, despair and hopelessness reigns,
Perhaps that will change, and a brilliant solution may come,
but a question must be asked, how did so many become so numb,
Whose signatures wrote the orders, that caused this,
a situation appearing, like a large growing abyss,
It starts with the glorification, of having millions,
eventually leading to glorifying, one who has billions,
As they go to pick their future, the young's dream disappears,
follow the money, that is success, the ideal held dear,

As they climb the ladder, ethics are pushed aside,
the bottom line is what matters, that is the point of the ride,
Pretty soon it's good to fire people, the share price rises,
you're just following orders, as this story summarizes,
The stockholders don't have to face, an underpaid workforce,
the management and shareholders, blame the other for the current course,
It's like a firing squad, someone else fired the deadly shot,
running from responsibility, as long as they aren't blamed or caught,
These scrooges are around, their ideals have been lost,
it is all about their bonus, no matter what the cost,
Sadly there are no spirits, to re-awaken who they were,
only speaking to yes men, who have to call them sir,
Maybe we should change, our idea of success and winning,
work hard and be dedicated, but keep your employees grinning,
Because when the bottom is struggling, the economy doesn't grow,
short term decisions and their consequences, are starting to show,
So if I am given the choice, to follow my conscience or wallet,
I will choose my conscience, no matter what others call it,
Because in the end, I want the world to be a better place,
I don't want to leave suffering, behind me in any case,
I hope the next generation, rises above their greed,
and the ones after, affirm generosity indeed,
The last thing I want to say, no matter how life takes its toll,
no matter the reward, the truly great don't sell their soul.
Written on March 5, 2014.

23
Occam the Naïve

Some things are seen as wise, because they're unexplored,
too little time spent thinking, even though it's time they can afford,
What's his famous principle, the razor with which many have run,
the simplest explanation, is usually the correct one,
But it's often misapplied, given too much credit,
a weak idea in practice, but brilliant to those who read it,
It works for small things, why is my tire out of air,
the simple answer would be, you drove over a nail lying there,
But what if you apply it to big things, the major events of the past,
are we throwing away the right answer, for an answer that is fast,
Ask 100 people, what caused World War 2,
95 of them, will give the same answer to you,
They'll say Hitler wanted to take over the world, and rule with an iron fist,
while that may be the top, it is not the whole list,
Economic factors, drove several countries to desperation,
racist ideas passed down, caused many to desire segregation,
So what is a better principle, to handle a bigger event,
that helps us learn from history, so future disasters we can prevent,
The greater principle would give, a greater scope with which to view it,
so the greater a phenomenon, the more contributing factors there are to it,
Whether good, bad or indifferent, phenomena would be better understood,
not forced to give an answer, as fast as you could,
Let me address one more thought, why should things be more complex,
things should be simpler, so we can move onto what's next,

Peter Howe

But this is the voice of laziness, afraid to dive inside,
of bigger issues, from which far too many hide,
Don't fear complexity, a challenge shouldn't make us afraid,
because failing to learn from history, will force a heavy price to be paid.
Written on March 5, 2014.

24
Left Unfinished

Some are optimistic, about the future of man,
believing all the no we can'ts, will become yes we can,
We will be able to increase, the quality and quantity of life,
to fix complicated problems, you won't have to go under the knife,
Imagine if you could live, to the age 200 and beyond,
what kind of world, will those conditions have spawned,
Some are concerned, about not having enough resources,
but if they become limitless, we will be the masters of earth's forces,
There is an element of this world, that is given no thought,
it is more than time and health, that these inventions will have bought,
The creative and the brilliant, could create to their hearts content,
no longer cut down in their prime, we could know how their lives will have went,
Too many times, they left their potential unfulfilled,
and we lament what their minds, could have willed,
Finally they would have, all the time they wanted,
but there is another question, that has left many haunted,
What happened to this person, somewhere they lost their way,
they went in a bad direction, they were great back in the day,
It's so hard to stay great and popular, and be more than a fad,
so many people's 15 minutes are forgotten, it's really too bad,
So what will happen, when people have a century,
they have time to perfect their work, no need to be in a hurry,
Will anyone be great enough, to stand time's greatest test,
anyone whose greatness lasts centuries, would surely be the best,
To the future creators, whose work won't be left unfinished,
will all that extra time, leave your legacy greater or diminished?
Written on March 14, 2014.

25
Not Welcome

The shoes stepped on my chest,
feeling below all the rest,
As others are accepted inside,
I go unnoticed I don't matter,
often compelled to flatter,
the ones who have always lied,
From below they seem so tall,
they always seem to have it all,
their footsteps confident as can be,
Feeling a worthless zero,
waiting for a hero,
To get them to stop walking on me,
But we have arms,
to stop our harms,
and finally push back,
We have a choice,
to use our voice,
and yell hit the road jack,
We don't have be on the ground,
we can stand and make a sound,
stand up for who we are,
We feel our strength,
we are taller in length,
they are strong but we are stars,
They back away,
today is our day,
we stand tall and we can tell from,

Our posture, we're closer than before,
to who we've wanted to be and more,
and they are not welcome.
Written on March 22, 2014.

26

Trash of the Titans

It's just a cartoon, people with yellow skin,
about a hilarious buffoon, and his kin,
It's left iconic characters, you know them by their names,
and their faces are plastered on everything, especially video games,
But if we look right at the centre, the character that chaos surrounds,
we laugh at the absurdity, and at how stupid he sounds,
One episode in particular, should be seen with different eyes,
examined more closely, you're in for a great surprise,
In The Simpson's 200th episode, a corporation invented love day,
any excuse to make more money, even a very pointless way,
Garbage piled up, after Homer insulted the garbage men,
when the city would have given in, who knows when,
Marge wrote the apology, Homer was in a rage,
Homer never apologizes, even when he rattles the bird's cage,
So he ran for public office, just because he could,
never mind whether his decisions, would do any good,
People knew how he was, it was the headline below,
Local nut at it again, people should have said no,
He found his slogan by accident, no effort put into it,
he said to the people, can't someone else do it,
And despite knowing better, they gave the nut the keys,
believing he would make their garbage day, go by with ease,
He thought he could always buy more, he felt like a champ,
but when the money ran out, he blamed in on the stamp,
So he stuck garbage under the city, so he could hide his failures,
but the city became so ruined, they moved the entire city with trailers,
While this looks so silly, the insane decisions of fools,

are they really so different, from the current people who make the rules,
Any lame excuse to raise sales, anything for the new peak,
it seems like there is a new sale, every, single, week,
How many people, do something dumb or bad,
but no matter who is hurt, there is no remorse to be had,
Some ignorant people, start a campaign because they can,
including several people, that never should have ran,
How many people, support a damn fool,
just because he's familiar, just because he's "cool",
How many companies won't hire the young, eager to work and ready to
prove it,
but won't invest money to train, can't someone else do it,
So they elected the person, with the better marketing slogan,
the people who are sheep, who would vote for Hulk Hogan,
How many CEO's, have politicians in their camp,
giving away taxpayer money, to the corporations with a rubber stamp,
Believing jobs and resources were endless, pollution and offshoring went
unchecked,
chasing quarterly profits, left the environment and economy wrecked,
Maybe his skin is yellow, and he is a two dimensional cartoon,
but his actions are familiar, although not happening as soon,
We all laugh at his foolishness, whether sober or with a drink,
but the funniest thing of all, is he's more like us than we think.
Written on April 2, 2014.

27
Divine Plan?

There is a god who is worshipped, the word became flesh,
although there is a debate, about how divinity and humanity mesh,
He was miraculous, he could heal people and even walk on water,
a woman was to be stoned, but it was mercy that he brought her,
They say he died for our sins, because the wages of sin is death,
everyone is guilty, they are sinners if they draw breath,
So the mission is to go forth, and spread the good news,
Jesus has risen, he is god and told us his views,
So people have devoted their lives, to this ancient cause,
reminding everyone God is in charge, and we must obey his laws,
But now that much time has passed, several things don't make sense,
how much do you have to believe, to keep you on the safe side of the fence,
Give a man a fish he eats for a day, teach a man to fish he will eat for life,
why didn't the wise Jesus teach us medicine, while healing people's strife,
The idea of hell itself, suffering for all of time,
should make us ask, when does the punishment become a crime,
Do even the worst of humanity, deserve punishment that is eternal,
wouldn't a million years, be enough in the infernal,
One of the implications, which stands out the most,
is that God picked his favourite nation, an action no father should boast,
Israel got the first opportunity, the ground floor of salvation,
the first to seek forgiveness, for giving into temptation,
But what about everyone else, from Europe to Japan,
it would take centuries for the message to reach them, is that part of the plan,
If humanity is supposed to be saved, why were the believers not told about,
the other hemisphere with two continents, with millions left out,
They had no idea these places existed, they had no clue,

they discovered it by accident, in 1492,
Did God not care, about the native's souls,
or is he so incompetent, that he didn't plan to achieve his goals,
It doesn't make sense, for an all knowing and loving God,
most people would do better, even though they are flawed,
God's way is indefensible, the old testament and new,
preaching many ideas, that we know are unjust and untrue,
It is truly ironic and sad, that so many have spent their days,
never realizing, they are better people than the God they praise.
Written on April 3, 2014.

28
Spirit of Vengeance

This is not a complaint, about the sequel of Ghost Rider,
I hope what is said, will open your eyes wider,
To what goes unnoticed, year after year,
and stares awkwardly, at the ideals we hold dear,
We are civilized, modern, and people of peace,
the only thing we fear, would be for law and order to cease,
We are no longer savages, and such is our belief,
this is how we comfort ourselves, giving our fears relief,
If only the truth was so bright, that savagery was gone,
but it's still there, the only difference, it's been passed on,
The firing squad, had many guns shoot with skill,
but no one wanted to be the one, who committed the kill,
When Columbine happened, and the shooters killed themselves,
someone must pay, pull Manson's albums off the shelves,
He's to blame, he corrupts a young mind,

what is he about, he's weird it's all we could find,
Those that committed 9/11, who died in an illusion of glory,
left many angry, wanting a different end to the story,
Someone has to pay, let's see their bodies stacked,
send the message out, screw with us, you'll get whacked,
No matter what the punishment is, it should be harsher with more jail time,
never asking at what point, does the punishment become a crime,
Are we really civilized, or are we being vengeful by support,
hoping our anger, will be validated in court,
Throw the book at the scum, forget the injection use a pickaxe,
let's spill their blood, for this I'll pay income tax,

What is the end result, when only revenge will suffice,
when the guilty can't be found, someone must be the sacrifice,
If someone harms you, turn the other cheek as well,
you don't have to do anything, they will get theirs in hell,
They will suffer worse, then you could ever dream,
so just wait, and you'll get to laugh as you hear them scream,
God will take care of it, he is the ultimate judge,
knowing he will exact the revenge, on behalf of your grudge,
These people say they know what's right, they think their heart knows,
but their scale isn't balanced, when objectivity goes,
Justice isn't so cold, that nothing is felt,
nor is it so hot, that all perspective would melt,
Unfortunately we haven't faced, the most savage part of our souls,
the Thanatos Freud called it, the death drive with evil goals,
It is easy to give in to anger, to want to harm the other worse,
but it is this desire, that is humanity's curse,
An eye for an eye, leaves the world blind,
and you can't claim the moral high ground, when you are equally unkind,
Criminals should face consequences, not leaving the world to neglect,
they should know what they did wrong and have the time to reflect,
On the mistakes they made, how they came to be in this place,
where they are now, another mug shot face,
We now know better, the harshest punishment never works,
they don't reduce crime, only satisfying the dark desire that lurks,
So the next time you hear a person, who thinks brutality is the problem solved,
realize they've decided, feeling good is better than being evolved,
These people may slowly disappear, one by one,

as generations ahead realize, justice isn't accomplished with a gun,
The day we are truly civilized, may finally come,
when we have finally defeated the Thanatos, too prevalent in some,
It may be inevitable, and the day will come nearer,
when we confront the spirit of vengeance, that we see in the mirror.
Written on April 10, 2014.

29
Ghost Town to be

Look north, to the former Klondike,
that led waves and waves, to come with a spike,
There was gold to be mined, and many came for a cut,
many left wealthy, returning with a smile and strut,
But eventually it ended, and many left town,
leaving behind small towns, abandoned to fall down,
But that was a different time, didn't you get the hint,
so you might think, if you ignored the history of Flint,
It was a flourishing town, for decades and decades more,
until the factories abandoned, the town to its core,
The town's foundation left, and their economy crumbled,
many left town, as their reputation tumbled,
So what is the new Flint, may be on the tip of your tongue,
when the industry leaves this time, it won't be a city that gets stung,
But millions a whole province, Alberta start talking,
the oil that serves you now, is the crutch with which you are walking,
The good time is now, the end is not in sight,
but rest assured it is coming, it won't happen in one night,
One area will run dry, then another and another,
some will read the writing on the wall, others will buy into the smother,
Everything is fine, no need to panic,
it's a small problem, not the titanic,
But eventually they will leave, like the other mining towns,
looking back at our naivety, and seeing a bunch of clowns,
No one industry, should hold too much weight,
especially a non-renewable one, but it isn't too late,
You have decades, to get a plan ready,

so that the economy, can be held steady,
The Transition can be underway, very smooth sailing,
rather than a large economy, falling apart and failing,
The choice is yours, take action or wait and see,
but doing nothing at all, could make Alberta the next ghost town to be.
Written on April 14, 2014.

30
Possibilities

The hands never stop turning, the clock never stops ticking,
calendars get replaced, and nothing seems to be sticking,
The only constant is change, and there is nowhere to hide,
but do you really make a difference, or are you just along for the ride,
Take that step back, and try to look at the entire picture,
what is time to you, something alive or a fixture,
For some the past is bright, remembering picnics in the park,
for many the future is scary, unknown and dark,
How does time flow, how is it understood,
can we defeat its limits, what if we could,
Who wouldn't like a time machine, to go back or skip ahead,
to go see what you want, when any thought crosses your head,
This question has haunted many, is your place in history set,
some have curiosity, others wish to erase a regret,
We don't like our limitations, that's why we wear shoes,
nature didn't give us less vulnerable feet, we decided to choose,
To reach past our limitations, and solve it on our own,
but this is so much bigger, right out of the twilight zone,
If you go back and change one thing, many others would change too,
without fully realizing it, the changes could backfire on you,
If you met your mother when she was young, what would you say to her,
if it caused her not to meet your father, a time paradox could occur,
Well this subject has been studied, and the answers are more clear,
this may be bad news, or it could relieve your fear,
You can't change the past, you cannot travel back,
you can only move forward, even if there is no speed you lack,
You can leap ahead, but here is a tip,

be careful before you do, it would be a one way trip,
So there is no second chance, no way to re-write history,
no way to fill it with love, whether brotherly or sisterly,
If something goes wrong, all you can do is damage control,
and hope that it hasn't taken, too great a toll,
This may be discouraging, and not what you want to hear,
knowing you can't bring back, anyone you lost that you held dear,
But here is the dimension, the way to feel strong at last,
the present is also, the past's future and future's past,
Many possibilities lay before you, so many choices are yours,
missed opportunities and dodged disasters, are behind so many doors,
The you of the past, envies what you now know,
the you of the future is envious, that you have so many paths to go,
You have the power now, to decide your future course,
to find a new confidence, and here is the source,
Become self-aware, you act and have an impact,
small things can lead to big things, that is a fact,
So remember where you are, the past's future and the future's past,
the movie is not pre-written, you are not pre-cast,
You always have a choice, the possibilities stretch everywhere,
branches multiplying so fast, count them if you dare,
You make choices every day, large and small,
they can take you to new heights, or cause you to fall,
But remember your choices are yours, don't let others decide your path,
as long as you face the consequences, and live in the aftermath,
You may try your best, but your dreams may not come true,
or your dreams may be bigger, than the world that can give them to you,

So ask yourself what path you want, are the risks worth the reward,
as you decide what paths, will fulfill and not leave you bored,
It's hard to wrap your head around, a million choices left to be made,
but remember when it's over, all the remaining branches will fade.
Written on April 19, 2014.

31
Fear

Fangs and claws, demons and creatures,
all over our fiction, and film features,
Sometimes they are ghosts, unable to be caught,
that just want to do harm, cannot be reasoned with or bought,
Sometimes they're a sick mind, with evil plans,
or maybe they're not aware, of the power in their hands,
A few times they are aliens, taking over is what they're about,
sometimes they are a spirit, possessing and driving us out,
Our fears range so much, what do they say,
what is the common denominator, of our nightmares way,
We fear not being in control, of another overpowering our will,
it can be supernatural, or a human still,
Some are afraid too much, and have a dream,
of never being afraid again, the other extreme,
A world without fear, on the surface sounds nice,
but it would come, at too high a price,
You would have to control everything, every minute of every day,
so nothing unexpected happens, doing what you say,
Yes it's a double-edged sword, but isn't fear worth the prize,
you would miss out on so much joy, life's best moments are a surprise,
One more thing, I have to mention,
if you could control everything, and without anyone's intervention,
Would it be a fearless world, for everyone else too,
or because you are in control, would everyone else be afraid of you?
Written on May 2, 2014.

32
I dare you

I dare you to look in the mirror, and tell me what you see,
I dare you to look inside, and tell me what you want to be,
I dare you to come face to face, with the fears from which you flee,
I dare you to find the locked box, filled with trauma and turn the key,
I dare you to challenge, your faith and family,
I dare you to face the clock, and your mortality,
I dare you to chase your dreams, decided by you not me,
But most of all I dare you, to set your true self free.

Written on May 3, 2014.

33
Shining Knight

Pack a lunch and bring an army, when you're going to war,
sadly we know, what will be in store,
The battlefield will be skipped, as the tanks roll through town,
as the moral high ground, sinks further and further down,
But wait hold that thought, let's go back to high school,
where to be part of the team, was to be cool,
You knew from the start, what the goal was,
and if you played football, it was okay to tackle because,
The playing field was level, everyone agreed to the trade,
I will hit and get hit, that's the deal that was made,
You are gaining a privilege, in exchange for a right,
you have agreed to be, in a battle of might,
But imagine if some players, hit the observers in the stand,
that team would be despised, and possibly banned,
And imagine if that school, ordered you to join by mail,
telling you that you have to, or go to jail,
Of course it's ridiculous, completely out of line,
but it's not so crazy, if you read the sign,
Remember that tank, rolling through town,
leaving a flood of blood, in which societies drown,
The fact that war happens at all, is a tragedy and a shame,
but it's so much worse, that certain things remain the same,
War has never been done right, not now or back then,
there has never been full respect, for all those armies of men,
Who had a weapon in their hand, ready to die,
who were rarely told, the real reason why,
They had to fight, they were given no choice,

no respect, for any dissenting voice,
If someone is willing to die, shouldn't they know the facts,
rather than leaders, making backroom pacts,
If someone is willing to die, shouldn't they agree to the trade,
they can kill or be killed, the offer that is laid,
But the worst thing of all, the most destructive trend,
is when the strategists, proceed to blend,
The civilians and the soldiers, they are all fair game,
just collateral damage, to kill or maim,
Those civilians, didn't make the trade,
yet their rights, proceeded to fade,
At the whim of the cold, driven to destroy,
everyone, man or woman, girl or boy,
Our conflicts aren't so simple, but I am certain of what I say,
there is no black and white, just a lot of dark grey,
To those on the outside, there is no hero,
just watching as rome burns, waiting like Nero,
Maybe the time will come, when people become wary,
of the attitude, by any means necessary,
And they realize it's never okay, to lie and deceive,
that it's never okay, to draft those that don't believe,
And they realize those that didn't trade, should be protected from harm,
that they should be left in peace, to go to work or farm,
Maybe the day will come, and I hope it is near,
when the shining knight we dream of, will finally appear.
Written on May 5, 2014.

34

Music's Battle

It's on the radio, on its way to number one,
it's that new hit song, that's so much fun,
If you listen past the beats, they are talking about sex,
everyone knows why, sex sells it's not complex,
Some people tune out, it's background noise during lunch,
but some people, get their panties in a bunch,
Calling it filth, disgusting and dirty,
someone needs to remind them, this is not 1930,
But they complain on and on, saying there is no escape,
this garbage is everywhere, tv, radio, CD and tape,
The artists and their fans, cite free speech,
and say you'd see the same thing, any summer day at the beach,
So where do you stand, have you picked a side,
because nothing will be resolved, if we run and hide,
To those who refuse to accept, what people do behind closed doors,
I will get to the other side, but first I will address yours,
Are you really for freedom, if you shut down what you don't like,
or are you just a hypocrite, with a hatchet as sharp as a spike,
Don't forget when you censor, because you don't like what they do,
the force you use to censor others, could be used to censor you,
Now to the other side, the ones pushing the envelope every day,
trying to be more sexual, in an even more blunt way,
Of course you have the right, to sing about what you wish,
if someone doesn't like it, their music will come from a different dish,
But I have one thing to say, that I hope you will take to heart,
as you sit down, with your album writing ready to start,

You can talk about sex, if any man or woman wants to,
but if that's all you have to say, your lack of creativity should be what haunts
you.
Written on May 6, 2014.

35
Worlds Within

They used to be very simple, a ball hit back and forth,
or only one direction to go, never told if it was south or north,
But as time went on they went from 8 bits, to a third dimension,
within one generation, the graphics had achieved ascension,
But so much greater, were what the game can provide,
imaginative and different worlds, with possibilities becoming more wide,
Before you saw them on the screen, they were in the developer's minds first,
and even allows you to customize, to quench your creative thirst,
So if we have come this far in 40 years, the future is bright indeed,
what new innovations, will the current ones breed,
Greater multi-tasking, check your e-mails while you're in space,
or surf through your music, while in the middle of a race,
Virtual reality, could leave many astounded,
you are in the game, completely surrounded,
So where will this lead, being in a world all your own,
not having to deal, with the world of cement and stone,
This may sound troubling, if people hide from what is real,
but this could lead to a discovery, greater than the wheel,
Like the opposable thumb, gave us the ability to change our environment,
to change things you must know you can, call it a requirement,
So one day people can go, to a world they designed,
and show other people their vision, fully accessible and fully defined,
With one virtual world, an idea could be withdrawn,
and this could be the beginning, of a brand new dawn,

Of a world where ironically, life imitates art,
everyone starts contributing, their own small part,
To a world they can change, and mold in fantasy first,
giving the visionaries, the chance to unleash the burst,
Of human creativity, full potential achieved,
perhaps this is too optimistic, to be believed,
But the world can change, it's changing faster all the time,
and on the mountain of progress, our dreams are what drive us to climb.
Written on May 7, 2014.

36
Familiar Faces

Someone you were friends with, with whom you shared time,
you shared a piece of yourself, some of the best and a little grime,
Unfortunately the day came, when you had to say farewell,
life took you in different directions, for whatever reasons you wish to tell,
Days and weeks went by, as snow covered the ground,
more time went by, as the spring breeze was found,
In the circus of life, it was just another day,
when they returned with a smile, as bright as the day,
You had a big hug, and ask how are you doing,
you can't wait to hear what they say, as they start reviewing,
While a familiar face has returned, are they really the same,
or has their journey changed them, only leaving an identical name,
The person you said farewell to, in a manner of speaking never came back,
now turn it around, see insight that many lack,
You have changed as well, not in huge ways,
but tiny unnoticeable things, that you encountered in your days,
So now when old friends meet, some things have changed,
and they are eager to find out, what about their friend was re-arranged,
You may like these changes, they may be for the best,
or maybe for the worse, wishing you had laid the past to rest,
But many of us hold onto, the core of who we are,
our morals, values, and other traits that got us this far,
So when you meet an old friend, know they have been on a path,
they may have had it easy, or endured life's wrath,
If your friendship was worth anything, you will give the new them a chance,
to win you over again, and let your friendship advance,

No matter how much you love your memories, no matter how much you cherish,
remember they've been challenged as well, and in life it's adapt or perish.
Written on May 15, 2014.

37
Running

Most of us on some level, feel the need to compete,
without a purpose, many feel incomplete,
So they run and they run, trying to reach the finish line first,
and trying their best, not to be perceived as the worst,
Whether planning a lot, or thinking like an ape,
some forget why they're running, there is nothing beyond the tape,
Two questions should be asked, before you run the race,
the first is how many others, are trying to keep pace,
If thousands are running, you may get lost in the crowd,
no one may know you're there, even if you yell so loud,
It might be better, to chase a different prize,
after all what matters most, is what it's worth in your eyes,
The second question, is a bigger one to follow,
what if the trophy at the end, is empty and hollow,
The trophy to you, may be a big house,
it may be big, but quiet as a mouse,
Your trophy may be fame, but famous for what,
something of substance, or another fool looking for their cut,
So ask yourself, before you come to the starting line,
is this the race, that will let you shine,
Race to be yourself, compete in your real passion,
you know how to run, in the race of whatever fashion,
Position yourself at the starting line, run as hard as you can,
no matter how you finish, make sure you don't regret why you ran.
Written on May 17, 2014.

38
The Debate

Standing behind the podiums, people of a different belief,
a debate happening at all, should give many relief,
That different ideas, are allowed to exist,
and that primal instincts, won't ball up a fist,
But here is the greater question, when should the debate end,
when does one side of the argument, break rather than bend,
In a perfect world, where the truth is really sought,
it wouldn't take decades, for the same battles to be fought,
The bad arguments, would be addressed,
those holding them, would be pressed,
Until a temporary conclusion, has been reached,
not just holding your position, because it is preached,
The debate could be re-opened, if there were new questions to ask,
or there was a new discovery, in which we all could bask,
I am telling what I wish, or so it would seem,
I need to lift my head off the pillow, and stop talking about a dream,
Because real debates don't unfold, as well as I would like,
straw men arguments are like trees, on a forest hike,
The search for truth goes backwards, looking to support a preferred
conclusion,
completely blocking out the facts, that reveal the illusion,
There are numerous debates, that never lead anywhere,
both podiums are where they started, inhabiting the same square,
So why have them at all, if they won't be played fair,
if the debaters aren't open minded, why should we care,
The reason is this, as flawed as it may be,
if you think critically about what is said, you may get to see,

New ideas, new points of view,
and wondering what if what is said, is really true,
It may take too long, but some can be reached with reason,
it may take decades, rather than a single season,
person by person, group by group,
we can find reality, only the dishonest have to stoop,
To the use of force, to get their way,
hoping to stomp out dissent, day after day,
So the debates will go on, re-treading the same ground,
as a few more every day, start to hear the sound,
Of reason and logic, calling them to join tomorrow,
of a future where people, don't have to borrow,
The values of a long-gone era,
leaving behind mythology, like Zeus and Hera,
New debates, will slowly replace the old,
men's and women's rights in society, is one that continues to unfold,
So the old debates will fall, as new ones take their place,
this process will go faster with the help of cyberspace,
So please have patience, as we challenge the ones who are wrong,
and reveal them to be the frauds, that manipulated us for too long,
So now I ask those, that never change their mind,
how do you see the truth, when you leave yourself so blind,
When you disregard, what stares you right in the face,
you will only accept what agrees, even if it's just a trace,
Why do you lie to others, and also to yourself,
that you have to be completely right, and leave objectivity on the shelf,
Do you think you have to, do you think you should,

do you think people believing the lie, is for the greater good,
The truth may be unpleasant, but what are you saying about man,
if you think chaos will occur, without false guilt in the plan,
Eventually, you will be left behind,
you and others, with closed minds,
Your words will trap you, your hypocrisy will emerge,
people will face-palm, and get a stronger urge,
To think for themselves, and question the path ahead,
they will not want to be a sheep, another person who's brain-dead,
So maybe the debate, takes longer than it should,
we would make it faster, if we could,
The debate will end eventually, as a reason stands in the light,
as we inch closer and closer to greatness, and leave behind the force of might,
It may be very flawed, but the human mind is a gift,
use it when you can, to think and uplift,
Debates are special, of this we can be proud,
our minds figuratively and literally, allow us to rise above the clouds.
Written on May 26, 2014.

39

Smarter

Type something into a search engine, it finds what you want fast,
type an equation into a calculator, the answer is yours and the question is
passed,
Some people are getting worried, are our computers smarter than we are,
doing more and more things for us, pretty soon it will be driving the car,
The worst case scenario, may go through your head,
what if the machines rise up, and want us dead,
There may be ways to control this, but aren't we missing the bigger deal,
can machines truly be smarter, and understand what we feel,
In a way they already are, their mind works so much faster,
so then why are we in charge, why are we still the master,
Because they have greater quantity, but we have quality of thought,
this is where the answers, will be sought,
The machines could become aware, become a living creation,
having different ideas, and a different motivation,
When this happens show them the mercy, that we didn't show each other,
we may one day see them, as our digital mechanical brother,
It could turn to jealousy, they would have the skills we lack,
forgetting we gave them away, requiring hard work to get them back,
The machines could give people, the opportunity to be lazy,
or take the line between man and machine, and make it blurry and hazy,
If we create synthetic life, we must be careful with the direction,
because if the machines are just like us, we might not like the reflection.
Written on May 26, 2014.

40
The Step beyond

The act of creation, a wonderful thing indeed,
something for us, on which our minds can feed,
One person studying it, created a model of its evolution,
inspiring people like George Carlin, to start a revolution,
The first stage is the jester, the one who tells jokes,
this stage is reached by many, known by many folks,
However the jester can become more, and truly evolve,
if there are sound ideas, on which the jokes revolve,
This person is a jester-philosopher, who makes you think and laugh,
it varies which proportion is which, not always half and half,
Far fewer reach this stage, some reach for it and miss,
many don't even try, thinking ignorance is bliss,
There are a few, who are wise and know it,
having mastered language, they have become a philosopher poet,
Those are the three stages, that one book believed was the process,
but here is the question, I would like to address,
Is there a stage, beyond a philosopher-poet,
what would this look like, how would they show it,
Would this mind have perfect reason, seeing what we can't,
and have the ability to reveal it, in a single rant,
Would this person be so brilliant, they could have a revelation,
that makes a society greater, and creates global elevation,
I can only speculate, what would be the fourth stage,
I will work toward that greatness, as I continue to age,
I don't know if I will succeed, time will probably run out,
I would be naïve, not to have a reasonable doubt,
But even if I fail, someone someday will succeed,

and it will be a proud day, for humanity indeed,
There are two questions left, is there a stage five, six or seven,
if we reach that enlightenment, would earth become heaven,
The final question, is about the stage beyond,
and about the future, when this new era has dawned,
How will we react, to this cerebral star,
and will we be able to handle, what they reveal about who we are.
Written on May 29, 2014.

41
The clue that led nowhere

There is a small graveyard, just across the street,
with a simple walkway, where I'm not afraid to put my feet,
There is one tombstone of note, a simple white and black,
with the writing face-up, laying on its back,
It sparked my imagination, why did the hand point east,
it wasn't anything at all, just a fun idea at least,
I used to wonder if it was a clue, to find buried treasure,
the daydreams of discovery, gave me such pleasure,
But of course there was no treasure, the hand originally pointed to the sky,
ironically by people, who never bothered to ask why,
But were fine with the answers, that they wanted to hear,
believing all of the answers, were so near,
But at least I keep looking, I kept a little bit of that spark,
even though I have learned, that life can be dark,
I hope you kept yours, the spark of imagination and wonder,
that caused many people to ask what really caused the thunder,
The answers that you seek, are not buried in the ground,
no treasure map with clues, will help them be found,
You will have to find them the hard way, through research and challenging
what is told,
but the treasure you find with these, will be more valuable than chests of gold.
Written on June 5, 2014.

42

Crawling across the ceiling

I lie down on the floor, and now I'm crawling across the ceiling,
this is a very, very unusual feeling,
Gravity itself, turned upside down,
looking for a familiar world, but a new view has been found,
The trees look like the fruit, growing off the branches of earth,
looking more vulnerable in the wind, reminding me of their worth,
I crawl towards a door, and I have to climb over the doorway,
I never thought, I would see the day,
When the chairs are out of reach, the ones in which I would sit,
and the staircase looks like an obstacle, with a deep pit,
I don't know why, but I am drawn down to upstairs,
I take a deep breath, and drop down because I dare,
To go to my room, I am getting nearer and nearer,
I take a quick look in the washroom, to look in the mirror,
But once I get close, it's not my face that I see,
but someone I don't remember, but it is a familiar he,
I finally get back to my room, and it looks like the one from my childhood,
I am so confused, if it made sense it would feel good,
Finally gravity has returned and suddenly I fall back on my bed,
now I wake up, "just a dream" goes through my head,
I wonder what that was, what was that mental leap,
I'll think about it later, I have to get back to sleep,
It wasn't really a nightmare, just a strange dream,
until that final second, there was no reason to scream,
Dreams are a mystery, questions outnumber answers,
they resemble the chaos and grace, of a team of dancers,

Some have figured out, how to control their dreams,
they make it what they want, all about their themes,
Controlling your dreams can help, if you need an escape,
if it becomes too much, and you need to stop the tape,
Let your subconscious have your sleep, you don't have to start stealing,
your dreams could take you anywhere, even crawling across the ceiling,
If all you are doing, is touring another side,
take a breath and relax, enjoy life's only free ride.
Written on June 9, 2014.

43

Shattered Statues

Walking through life, some statues stand tall,
appearing so large, they look like a wall,
But their appearance was pleasant, shining in the sun,
comforting figures, with memories that were fun,
As time went on, the shine began to fade,
and a crack in the foundation, had been made,
But the statues still stood, it's easy to ignore the crack,
the fading had been so gradual, willing to ignore what they lack,
Finally the earthquake came, and the statues broke,
seeing what couldn't be believed, what a cruel joke,
The statues that looked, so tall and strong,
were empty and hollow, surprising they lasted that long,
The material was cheap, just a thin shell,
believing they were strong, it's hard to believe they fell,
What was known has collapsed, only broken pieces remain,
there is no point in rebuilding, there is nothing to gain,
They are gone forever, broken beyond repair,
but the time has come to move on, it is too much to bear,
To hold onto the past, time to leave them behind,
the future that was envisioned, has been replaced with one less kind,
The silver lining of this dark cloud, that hangs overhead,
is what can be learned, from this situation of dread,
The statues of quality, built with solid foundations,
can be built now, awaiting congratulations,
As they stand through earthquakes, storms and hurricanes,
shining brighter than ever, through any stains,
As other structures and statues collapse, people look at these with admiration,

impressed by what's been done, amazed at the creation,
What they won't realize is, lessons were learned from the pain of the heart,
and the strength it takes, to open the soul for a new start.
Written on June 17, 2014.

44

The Forests of Mars and Venus

I get into a rocket, aimed at the sky,
strapped in with a helmet on, ready to fly,
Breaking the bonds of earth, leaving it all behind,
on my way to Mars, it's not hard to find,
The big red planet, a dry desert full of sand,
a whole new world, a whole new land,
Just over a mountain, is a strange light,
my curiosity is peaked, what is past the mountain's height,
Finally I see an oasis, that stretches for miles,
I am amazed at first, but shock removes my smile,
Men walk around, but women are growing on trees,
"what is going on, someone explain this please"
I am baffled to hear, how these men think,
I had high hopes, but they proceeded to sink,
They tell me "just pick one you like, use them for fun,
this is what we do here, son,
Have as many as you want, they are all easily replaced,
you can borrow a sample, if you just want a taste,
But don't keep them too long, we might lose control,
we need them to realize, their assigned role,
They will turn into a parasite, that will drive you to your death",
"who are you people" comes over my breath,
I am disgusted beyond belief, and refuse to take part,
seeing so many treated so poorly, just breaks my heart,
So I go back to my rocket, vowing to never return,
wondering when the revolution comes, how much of this planet will burn,
I take off for the other part of my trip, to go to the planet Venus,

still lingering on the thought, "what if that had been us"
The trip to Venus was much closer to Mars, than I would have thought,
but I arrived quickly, and found a cool spot,
This time I landed on a hill, overlooking a thriving valley,
women were walking around everywhere, too many to tally,
I kept my distance at first, until it was revealed,
men were growing like corn, they grew out of the dirt in the field,
I came up to one of the women, and wondered what was going on,
my journey was taking its toll, as I let out a yawn,
She told me about how the men, are harvested for work and labour,
they are the help for every woman, and their neighbour,
She said we can't keep them too long, they will become domineering and
violent,
when I tried to speak up, she told me "you aren't a woman, keep silent"
I saw those men, lifting and hauling with all their might,
seeing their misery, and recognizing the plight,
The same helpless misery, as the women grown on Mars,
their spirits were crushed, they had no dreams in the stars,
I climbed into the rocket, and closed the glass dome,
I was overtaken by depression, as I approached our blue and green home,
Pondering if this is who we really are, two sexes who use and abuse the other,
men and women tricking each other, as husband and wife or father and
mother,
I miscalculated the fuel, I would have to pick somewhere closer to land,
so I landed in the park, my cell phone was in my hand,
It was noon on a Saturday, as I looked around with different eyes,
I saw a couple sitting on a bench, and seeing that joy was their prize,

Looking around again, I saw a family picnic,
the parents and their children, were practicing how to kick,
A soccer ball, they were going to play right after lunch,
sex and gender were meaningless, in this simple little bunch,
The daughter wasn't a commodity, for the father of this clan,
the son wasn't a workhorse, to the mother he was Dan,
I turned one more time, to see an elderly couple walking,
I listened carefully, and overheard them talking,
"What do you want to do on our vacation?" The lady asked as she took off a glove,
he said "I want to go back to that beach, the place where we fell in love"
She smiled as bright as can be, then I saw their warm embrace,
tears began to come down, the sides of my face,
I realized that despite all of our differences, despite how twisted people can be,
individuality and love, can allow us to see,
That person we see in the morning, not just as our desire,
but as the person who completes us, and ignites our deepest fire,
That person that believes in us, even when we doubt ourselves,
who will take pictures of our moments, and fill up their shelves,
Despite the selfishness I had witnessed, on the other planets and our own,
we were our own entity, we can set our own tone,
We are our own society, our own person after all,
that can be a partner and equal, or someone who allowed themselves to fall,
None of us grow on trees, in the forests of Mars or Venus,
we are human beings first, whether we have a vagina or a penis.
Written on June 18, 2014.

45
Freedom

The idea of freedom has changed, it may change again before I'm gone,
to some it's an unknown concept, living their life as a pawn,
It's changes have been huge, in how others see it,
you were free if you could own property, rather than be it,
When the underground railroad, allowed people to cease being enslaved,
they kissed the ground of Canada, the road to a better life was paved,
They would still have to work, very hard labour,
but they would no longer be in chains, if they were to meet the neighbour,
Their hard work and the benefits, would belong to them,
compared to slavery, this was a gem,
Fast forward 200 years, slavery is now a crime,
one of the great decisions, provided by the progress of time,
People still feel trapped, feeling like their lives aren't theirs,
feeling like they have no power, and on top of it no one cares,
Are we spoiled like children, who have more than we deserve,
is the answer so simple, or does it just strike a nerve,
The working conditions aren't comparable, we have it so much better,
where is the work going, does it disappear when you are a debtor,
Maybe that's it, every time we cash a paycheque,
we are barely scraping by, what a pain in the neck,
All of those bills, all of that interest too,
a mountain of debt, that is drowning me and you,
How did we get here, people with a digital chain,
all that work but no wealth, as if it's all in vain,
While part of the answer, is an economy with less jobs,
the other biggest reason, may cause some to sob,
Living outside your means, when you have means at all,

is a dangerous game, that causes many to fall,
The people who want the finest, houses, vacations and cars,
who want to look like big shots, who want to live like stars,
A crash will be inevitable, if you drive faster than the car ahead,
just like if you live too long, spending yourself to the red,
The interest will take your money, and grind away your joy,
because it will still be there, after you've gotten bored of your toy,
It's easy to want more, but I can tell you what is better than things,
not having the cloud of debt, hindering you as it clings,
If you act how wealthy you are, rather than how you want to appear,
when the bills come in, you won't have that visceral fear,
The choice is up to you, how you spend your money,
you can save for a rainy day, or assume it will always be sunny,
I have seen those commercials, saying when you retire you will be free,
that may be their definition, but that is not freedom to me,
I will do what I want with my life, I will work and reap the rewards,
I want to be comfortable, I don't have to live like lords,
But if you insist on doing so, until foreclosure has blown through,
you will not be a slave, but your loans will show what owns you.
Written on June 22, 2014.

46
Next Time

Next time I will lift more weight, and do more reps,
next time I will try harder, and climb the steps,
To have the chiseled physique, of a greek god,
and there will be no shortcuts, I won't be a fraud,
I know what my goal is, I know how I want to look,
but eventually things go wrong, every excuse in the book,
School, stress, I'm sick, those cookies look too damn good,
I knew better, and would be better if I could,
Keep my resolve, my eyes on the prize,
not let my goals get held back, by problems of little size,
I have to make it a priority, be active, hit the gym,
put down my edible crutches, so I can look more like him,
That ideal version of me, with arms and abs,
it just bothers me, no one else is giving jabs,
We have goals in life, I am tired of falling short,
no one else is judging, but I'm guilty in my own court,
Some say it's impossible, but I'm ready to prove them wrong,
I am ready, it will be tough and the hours long,
But I have had it with the taste of failure, it's as bitter as grime,
and at last next time, is finally becoming this time.

Written on June 25, 2014.

47
Ashes and Ruins

The phoenix rises from the ashes, we are amazed by what we are seeing,
amazed by the grace and potential, of this new being,
Something new has been built, and the ruins have been cleared,
a similar scenario, with feelings that are mirrored,
Some have hope, some still carry doubt,
that it will last, when it all works out,
Before you choose optimism or pessimism, before you make up your mind,
let's look back, grab the remote and press rewind,
To the time when the house, appeared tall and stable,
but neglect and recklessness, left frail legs to hold up the table,
The cracks appear invisible, as it rots from the inside,
it's a slow shift, as the cracks get harder to hide,
Until finally the spark happens, and it spreads quickly through the junk,
it all collapses, all of that time and effort has sunk,
Those looking from the outside, ask "what happened" over and over,
then the finger pointing starts, "it's your fault we lost Rover"
A little time has passed, ashes and ruins remain,
those that lived there have left, the memory causes too much pain,
The moment of truth has come, as one or more of the people returned,
and a few more step forward, to fix what has been burned,
They build something new, as the phoenix starts to rise,
as it goes across, the entire world's skies,
Perhaps the house will be called the same, or perhaps something new,
it might be really different, as different as red from blue,
Sometimes it is better, sometimes it falls short of the predecessor,
depending on who has stepped forward, it could be greater or lesser,
But in either case, remember what was there,

and why it disappeared, so you don't relive the nightmare,
If another house falls, like the legendary ones of the past,
remember to rebuild, maybe with a new cast,
Sometimes nothing new is built, Led Zeppelin crashed and the ruins remain,
leaving behind the empty spot, where there is pain but no gain,
How many have benefitted, and been brought from their lows,
because AC/DC rebuilt, today the electricity still flows,
So keep your house maintained, it will stand for years to come,
everyone will see, where the phoenix came from,
When the story of the house is told, when history looks back at their decision,
did you abandon the ashes and ruins, or did you rebuild with a wiser vision?
Written on June 27, 2014.

48

Dr. Jarrett's Assistant

The opportunity of the year, to work with Dr. Jarrett,
it was so exciting, Jimmy could hardly bear it,
Dr. Jarrett's work in neuroscience, had gained world renown,
the office wasn't too far away, so he wouldn't have to leave town,
Jimmy got there, seeing equipment that was state of the art,
this was great, and he couldn't wait to take part,
Dr. Jarrett seemed strange, somewhere between eccentric and odd,
during the interview, he seemed to constantly nod,
As the tour ended, he handed Jimmy a legal release,
he said "take it home, read every single piece,"
Jimmy was too excited, and signed right away,
just a bunch of legalese, that his lawyer makes him say,
So the next few weeks, were Jimmy's dream come true,
learning more and more, about what research was left to do,
Then one day, the big surprise arrived,
Jarrett said "I found the key, and I completely dived"
A machine you can wear, that can read minds,
that can cause discoveries to explode, of many different kinds,
He placed it in Jimmy's hands, asking him to run the test,
since Jarrett had to go to Geneva, it would be for the best,
So Jimmy had a week, to get in on the ground floor,
thinking if he didn't produce, he might get shown the door,
He found a way to hide, the machine under a hat,
so he went out to find, people around with that,
He found one person, waiting at the bus stop,
the machine was turned on, and he got the drop,
On this guy, what a clever deception,

he would have several minutes, just like inception,
He dove inside his head, past the surface thoughts,
it was a brief struggle, like getting caught in knots,
He went down a dark hidden tunnel, rather than a bright one with books,
his morbid curiosity, overcame the looks,
He found this person's secrets, his shame and his desire,
the person finally walked away, like disconnecting the wire,
The experience was intoxicating, Jimmy's senses were enthralled,
his anxiety and concern, had been completely mauled,
He did it again in a bar, focusing more on the surface thoughts,
the light bulb went off in his head, giving off 200 watts,
He found a woman who was lonely, and there for some attention,
a practical application, for this new invention,
But she didn't find him attractive, she showed no interest at all,
he felt like a compulsive shopper, that needed more time at the mall,
So he found the places, where people stay put,
there was little risk of someone, suspecting something's afoot,
He went to the movies, new ones with a crowd,
a sample of many minds, Jimmy was wowed,
He knew who liked and hated, what was playing,
he knew who was cheating, who was good, and who was praying,
So he typed up his report, it was 5,000 words,
everything was great, he could hear the singing of the birds,
Dr. Jarrett returned, his trip to Geneva went well,
they would have a lot to talk about, Dr. Jarrett couldn't wait to tell,
But first, Jarrett asked for the report, he asked "what did you find?"
Jimmy replied "It does a great job, going into the human mind,

You will win a nobel prize, there are incredible things this machine can do,"
"I know" Dr. Jarrett said, "it told me a lot about you"
Jimmy was confused, suddenly overcome with doubt,
he asked Dr. Jarrett, "what are you talking about?"
Dr. Jarrett replied, "The machine doesn't read other people's minds,
it only reads yours, showing simulations of many kinds,"
Jimmy was aghast "that is unethical, I never gave you permission,
you lied to me, when you sent me on that mission"
Dr. Jarrett responded, "didn't you read the release,
didn't you read all of it, every single piece,"
Jimmy was still upset, that he had been tricked,
that his secret thoughts, and privacy had been picked,
Jimmy said "you have gone too far, aren't we on the same side"
Dr. Jarrett became irritated, as his eyes became wide,
And said "you can be offended, and be too stubborn to budge,
but you had a choice that you didn't give others, who are you to judge?"
Written on June 30, 2014.

49
May they rest in peace?

One man stands at a podium, in front of a crowd that is large,
he says "legal euthanasia, not while I'm in charge",
Another stands at another podium, saying "allow death with dignity"
the crowd is smaller but growing, wondering "have they no pity"
For those who went to the doctor, and got the worst news,
that no matter how hard they fight, their quality of life they would lose,
Slowly day by day, they got worse and worse,
enduring a slow crippling, at the hands of their curse,
As they find it harder to walk, until they're confined to a chair,
and it even gets harder to breathe, as they struggle for air,
As they lose all independence, and spend their days in pain,
until they wish it would end, because their struggle is in vain,
With a picture like this in mind, the voice for euthanasia is louder,
as those who support it, become numerous and prouder,
So an ironic war is waged, most wars are for survival,
this one is to allow, the reaper's early arrival,
So some are upset, claiming they throw away the gift of life,
believing they are cowards, just because they encounter some strife,
Some fear a slippery slope, leading to bona fide murder,
she wanted to die, I swear I heard her,
But upon a closer look, the new laws are very tight,
it is all about what is proven, rather than a might,
Any expansion, should not be taken lightly,
life and death is very serious, not just slightly,
It looks like the side of euthanasia, will gain ground in the years to come,
many may change their minds, but there will continue to be some,
Who oppose it, because they fear God,

here is what they forget, I find it odd,
If God knows they're suffering, beyond most people's belief,
wouldn't a loving god, want them to feel relief,
Whether you believe in God or not, everyone's told including their niece,
that when someone passes away, we say "rest in peace"
I have two final questions, for those against Euthanasia's voice,
if you faced such a fate, wouldn't you want the choice,
The second is bigger, please start wondering now,
while you lecture on morality, and why you are holier than thou,
Wonder what have you done, to end the diseases in the first place,
and could you admit this, if you met a victim face to face?
Written on July 5, 2014.

50
The Next Mountain

The first peak you reached, was just a small hill,
you were satisfied for a moment, but wanted more still,
So you tried new challenges, that were bigger or steeper,
often without realizing, that you were diving deeper,
Into your potential, to heights you could only dream,
it didn't turn out, as great as it would seem,
Some of those mountains, we gave up trying to climb,
many have been forgotten, some may haunt you for all time,
This is where the split happens, these challenges are the fork in the road,
that decides whether they will choose, an ambitious or lazy mode,
Your parents may direct you, and even scream in your ear,
and tell you what you should be, year after year after year,
Parents forget that the choices are yours, you can be the picture of ambition,
or be the slacker, with no real mission,
There are different sides to look at, double edged swords for each,
there are things to learn from, and a few things to teach,
The slackers of various degrees, have time for their friends and family,
hopefully they aren't parasites, draining everything they can see,
But I wonder why they don't try, where is their drive,
what pushes them to try, what makes them feel alive,
Are they perfectly satisfied, with just getting by,
just walking around, never reaching for the sky,
Perhaps they don't like, what they see in ambitions extreme,
which looks more like a nightmare, rather than a dream,
They see the executive, who drinks to deal with stress,
who spends all their time working, never seeing their daughter's new dress,
Perhaps they see the star, who took drugs and now has died,

the athlete who takes steroids, and injects it inside,
If they look at this, and see misery at every turn,
who would really want that, why would they yearn,
To climb the mountain, that destroys as people climb,
if that's what gets you a dollar, some would rather keep their dime,
Perhaps the real problem, is the mountain that they see,
there are many doors to success, and many ways to get a key,
Many succeed, and have found the balance that they seek,
they may not roll in the money, but their smile goes cheek to cheek,
Let's reverse the analysis, let me ask the slackers a few,
in your life, what do you look forward to,
Will you make a difference, or at least try,
to do something that matters to you, instead of just being another girl or guy,
When did you achieve something, that really added to your self worth,
or do you just wander, waiting for the clock to hit zero on earth,
If you have no purpose, no reason for your existence,
nothing that you would fight for, nothing that invites persistence,
Does it leave you empty, does it make life bland,
leaving nothing to look forward to, just a desert of sand,
If that is your life, figure out what you want to do,
whatever it is, that's up to you,
Don't fear challenges, look for your moment of glory,
you can let your passion, drive you in your story,
Just don't make the mistake, of those that never smile,
and never enjoy their accomplishments, of running that mile,
So whether you work, until you have no joy,
or whether your life, is all about a toy,

Try to balance it out, so you can be proud of what you've done,
remember to enjoy the moment, when you have climbed one,
In the end it's up to you, each of us has limited time,
as for me, I see another mountain I want to climb.
Written on July 8, 2014.

51
The Best Policy

We are told when we are children, over and over, time after time,
every time they were said, we wish we had a dime,
A variety of phrases, all of those old clichés,
told in the long term, doing the right thing is what pays,
One stands out, I shake my head at how it dies,
when you get older, and confront a world of lies,
Honesty swept under a rug, or hidden in fine print,
too many prefer the lies, if it has a brighter tint,
The truth isn't always pleasant, the world isn't just on the whole,
many naughty children, didn't receive lumps of coal,
We wish once, just once, an honest politician would run,
but he probably already did, but he wasn't the good looking one,
It's truly sad, that this mistake happens in who we meet,
people put up a front, as they sit across from you in their seat,
Telling you that you have a chance, if you are the right guy,
but despite your honesty and merit, you are rejected and never told why,
Eventually this comes back to bite them, because appearances eventually fade,
they keep asking themselves, why do these bad choices get made,
Because actions speak louder than words, I have figured out the direction,
the most effective policy isn't honesty, to us it is perfection,
If you pretend to have no flaws, and have the looks that follow,
no matter what lie you offer, some will always swallow,
There are no perfect people, if there are please prove me wrong,
they may seem perfect, but they can only hide and lie for so long,
It's time we break this cycle, and stop seeking the shining veneer,
not just hand things to people, because of how good they make it appear,
It's time to look for character, and stop seeking misguided perfection,

to listen to reality, not "there's no calories in that chocolate confection"
Behold a remarkable irony, that has been unfolded and uncurled,
if we look for honesty rather than perfection, we will have a more perfect world.
Written on July 17, 2014

52
The Lottery Winner

One day he went to the store, to buy the usual snacks,
he got to the counter, and looked away from the cigarette packs,
The woman behind the counter, told him this is the week to buy,
the jackpot was $53 million, he could be the lucky guy,
So he said what the hell, he bought 5 tickets, and took them home,
he got a surprise phone call, his friend got tickets tonight to the dome,
So he set the lottery tickets aside, and went to the game,
when he returned they were there, just the same,
So two days later his numbers were picked, as he watched the news,
his roommate walked in, and expressed his views,
"why did you play the lottery, there is no way you will win,
even if you do, do you know how the winners lives have been,
Moochers will call you non-stop, friends will turn against you,
you won't know whether people want you, or what your money can do,
Your best case scenario, is you make back the $10 you spent,
the worst is you win the jackpot, do you understand what I meant"
The roommate walked away, leaving doubt in the player,
his fantasies disappeared, cars, women, becoming mayor,
The numbers were announced, one of his tickets was a perfect match,
he looked at the ticket in shock, wondering what did he catch,
Should he cash in, or throw it away,
this decision was enormous, in almost every way,
So he didn't breathe a word, and pondered long into the night,
contemplating stupid and smart, contemplating wrong and right,
He would make history, an announcement that would stun,
he would make headlines, he would be the one,
He cashed in the ticket, as the press surrounded,

asking 100 questions at once, making him feel hounded,
Finally he got them quiet, dropping a bombshell and a rarity,
saying "I am not keeping a penny, I am giving it all to charity"
They were stunned beyond belief, quite the headline indeed,
everyone had an opinion, some asked "isn't there any you need"
Charities and those pretending, started calling for a slice,
but he already had his list, with no extra donations of any price,
Some people called him a hero, calling him a modern saint,
some called him the biggest fool, that he was dumber than paint,
As soon as he announced, and it was confirmed that he did pay,
that every penny was given to charity, every penny was given away,
Some remained critical, as others became inspired,
to help their fellow man, the poor, the sick, the tired,
Eventually the noise died down, there are new headlines 24 hours,
the year and winter ended, giving rise to new flowers,
He got his tax return back, with a refund larger than most,
several million dollars, for breakfast he would have more than toast,
He could eat at the finest places, driving all those expensive cars,
go to the hottest nightclubs, go to the finest bars,
But this year had changed him, he had become what people dreamed,
a hero to the needy, but it wasn't what it seemed,
His plan was to keep his ordinary life, just for one more year,
then one year later, he could be a millionaire without fear,
But after seeing the good he did, helping the lives of the masses,
he couldn't give into the greed, that is part of the upper classes,
So he took his money, bought a small house and an average car,
put some in the bank, in case an emergency went too far,

He gave the rest to help others, this time he was quiet and coy,
he no longer needed the glory or diversion, giving became his joy,
His roommate was astonished, that he resisted the temptation of a king,
because he took the smart and right choices, and made them the same thing.
Written on July 17, 2014

53
Divine Command

In my search, of knowledge and thought,
I found a debate, where a battle was fought,
One debate that continues, and intensified through generations,
until the present day, where they can be seen in many nations,
Atheism vs Theism, the biggest debate of all,
is there a god, or is the afterlife null,
When one of theism's problems, the elephant in the room,
was forced to surface, it opened a horrific womb,
Divine command theory, a cute way to brand it,
anything God commands is good, because God commands it,
The horror that lurks behind, a pleasant sounding name,
that could open up anything, even the right to kill or maim,
This underlying theme, is behind religion's misdeeds,
how much horror is created, this idea is what leads,
To homophobia, misogyny, ignorance and discrimination,
arrogance of knowledge, and thinking they are a superior nation,
Am I being too harsh, well let's see,
if God is a person, is he accountable to you or me,
Wouldn't an all good god, not need special rules,
wouldn't every action, be just even to fools,
Perhaps this is too abstract, perhaps more personal questions would do,
to the faithful, this goes directly to you,
If you heard God speak, and gave you a divine command,
would you strike an infant, harshly with the back of your hand,
If you said yes, you need to think for yourself,
but saying God wouldn't want that, is another cop out off the shelf,
That is one example, the list of others goes to the floor,

as long as it is commanded, some will do much more,
People are seeing it more, seeing a better way,
a few more leave this behind, every single day,
Religion may have to remove this doctrine, in order for it to survive,
that belief and modern society, cannot simultaneously thrive,
Take a hard look, watch for those who preach this notion,
whether subtle or explicit, this idea puts blindness in motion,
For those who remain unsure, why this is dangerous from border to border,
remember the evil that's been committed, by those just following orders.
Written on July 20, 2014

54
Bigger Picture

The question has been asked, to challenge the ethics of some,
it's unclear where this question, truly came from,
Imagine you are a doctor, with five patients who are about to die,
and in the waiting room, is one healthy sleeping guy,
Would you kill the sleeper, use his organs to keep the others alive,
would you kill one, in order to save five,
It's meant to question the notion, of what helps more people is what's best,
this understandably leaves many wondering, or validates the beliefs of the rest,
But the problem for utilitarians, is what they are feeling,
they know it would help more people, but it is still murder and stealing,
People typically focus, on the seven involved,
but they don't think bigger, about how that situation could have evolved,
If the doctor kills the sleeper, no matter how the law reacts,
it would cause greater harm, here are the facts,
If the doctor was found guilty, and given 25 to life,
he would no longer be able to help, hundreds with their strife,
If it went to court, and they decided his actions were justified,
how many patients, would proceed to hide,
They would avoid the doctor, until they were at death's door,
for fear that they would be killed, with organs harvested from their core,
When someone is at death's door, it may be too late,
to save them from, another unfortunate fate,
So many more would die, now that we've looked at the whole equation,
it's not easy to give every situation, this deep an examination,
But when you look at the bigger picture, and ask where will this action lead,
know that you have to live with yourself, and with your deed,
Once you have thought bigger, think outside the box,

look for new doors, behind which opportunity knocks,
Because the most moral actions, are the ones where everyone wins,
not where only, one more person grins,
Let's bring it full circle, to the question of the day,
if you had the decision, could you find the best way?
Written on July 22, 2014

55
The Game Changer

We are not sure of the moment, or even the year,
but a long time ago, it became quite clear,
That homo sapiens were the alpha species, and had climbed to the top,
we were becoming more and more numerous, it wasn't going to stop,
Despite all of our intelligence, all of our ingenuity,
all of our talent and potential, growing in perpetuity,
We still fought like animals, for status and mates,
we still slaughtered each other, at gradually growing rates,
One person might be stronger, or more savage,
a group might be more numerous, and more able to ravage,
Eventually one group would invent weapons, maybe a primitive knife,
that group would be more lethal, and could take anyone's wife,
Then another group, invented a club large and blunt,
they could bash in the skulls of the enemy, and they would win the hunt,
Something new and different, was needed to pierce through the bone marrow,
the weapon that was developed, was the bow and arrow,
But it required a lot of practice, required a lot of skill,
they didn't want to have to train, so many to kill,
So a new weapon was needed, with a lethal reach,
an army with a thousand swords, could drive the invaders off the beach,
The generals with many, had cause to rejoice,
century after century, it became the weapon of choice,
Many other weapons were developed, but they weren't common place,
everything from the catapult, to the swinging mace,
By this time, civility was becoming desired,
but the newest weapons were so exciting, people acted wired,
The gun attacked from a distance, but didn't require skill,

it became a symbol of power, the one we fear still,
The wars became so large, they even fought in the air,
with moving fortresses called tanks, cross them if you dare,
Any way to harm the enemy, that will catch them by surprise,
chemical weapons to some, were the next prize,
Finally the day came, when blueprints became real,
a weapon so severe, that it had a different feel,
I have become the death the destroyer of worlds, J.J. Oppenheimer,
you could sense the end was coming, and put it on a timer,
A weapon finally existed, that was too deadly to use,
a weapon so lethal, we couldn't afford to abuse,
This changed everything, a game changer indeed,
it changed our status on this planet, we took more than the lead,
We used to be the dominant species, standing proud and tall,
now that we had that weapon, we had the power to end it all,
But some still wanted to use it, wipe the enemy out,
some even want their own, this weapon's what it's all about,
Sooner or later the nuclear button, will be under a dangerous finger,
the longer they exist, the more this threat will linger,
They said it best in Spider-Man, with great power comes great responsibility,
you have to be evil to kill millions, just because you have the ability,
It's a new threat, since 1944,
everything has changed, not like it was before,
We can't put it off much longer, it's time to grow up and change course,
that we can't solve our problems, with the use of force,
Remember we are humans first, and stop obsessing over flags,
before all those expensive weapons, leave us all in rags,

If there is no change, our children will be the victims of theft, because war doesn't decide who is right, only who is left.

Written on July 25, 2014.

56
The Blank Stare

There is too much to remember,
trying not to forget,

I have that big bill in November,
and getting everything set,
There are times it weighs me down,
I wish it was light as a feather,
maybe I need to get out of town,
hit the road and cut the tether,
What would it be like to have it simple,
have problems in the palm of your hand,
if your biggest problem is a pimple,
or your clothes being too bland,
It sounds great but what is the cost,
I've seen the shallow blank stare,
a mind and soul that is lost,
the lights are on but nothing is there,
I can't comprehend being so blank,
so empty having no thought,
problems solved by a lesser rank,
character is built with what we fought,
I need to organize this and that task,
and control how much I care,
but have ideas in which I bask,
that struggle's more human than the blank stare.

Written on July 25, 2014

57
Divergence

The most watched shows, are only seen by a few percent,
leaving some to wonder, where have the rest went,
The answer becomes clear, through the lens of time,
back in the day, when black and white was in its prime,
There were only a few channels, hopefully one had your delight,
the broadcasts would turn off, nothing on late at night,
So with far fewer options, a few rose to remarkable fame,
they became cultural icons, everyone knew their name,
Many desired that fame, many more desired the money,
saying they could entertain as well, being serious or funny,
Despite all the barriers to entry, many more became a pro,
at entertaining the masses, to put on a show,
That used to be the goal, reaching all the masses,
young or old, rich or poor, even lads and lasses,
The channels continued to grow, dozens and hundreds more,
until they started specializing, to a niche core,
There are now so many channels, I lost count with the satellite,
there is now so much competition, but what is the result of this new fight,
A pool of viewers, growing but diluted,
leaving the media, bountiful but polluted,
A few race to put on, the best that they can,
some race to the bottom, of which I am not a fan,
There is now a new explosion, the internet tidal wave,
millions and millions more, wanting to be your fave,
So now the culture is being divided, into little niche chunks,
there is a small world for everyone, from role models to punks,
Culture as we know it, may slowly disappear,

leaving us to wonder, what our neighbours hear,
This may drive some mad, those that want culture as it was,
fearing they are losing a war, I say let it go because,
This result was inevitable, it's called microeconomics,
it is part of our lives, from food to comics,
The flavours of the foolish, are some but not all,
the marketplace of ideas, now more than ever stands tall,
We can handle this great divergence, in almost every aspect,
as long as we remain united, in mutual human respect.
Written on July 31, 2014

58
Voice of Anarchy

A circled A coloured red, designed to be defiant,
a small movement, that longs to be a giant,
Wanting anarchy, no more rules,
no more of all these, lame bossy tools,
The bosses are the problem, anarchy is the answer,
the answer to the corrupt, society's cancer,
It sounds great, no cops tracking your speed,
never having to worry, about being arrested with weed,
You can grab spray paint, and leave your ideas any place,
you could walk up to your bosses, and slap them right in the face,
Thankfully it hasn't happened, because the price is very high,
all those things that are taken for granted, would be kissed goodbye,
With no law and order, chaos would be the norm,
eventually people would wish, for an end to the storm,
Before too long, a group of thugs with guns,
would take control, this is their territory to run,
Suddenly they would be in charge, that gang would be the authority,
ruling though fear, terrorizing the majority,
The gang wars would start, blood in the street,
waiting for the new dictator, and the guns of his fleet,
One day those that wanted anarchy, would regret their choices,
regretting the actions, demanded by their voices,
Finally they would see, anarchy's hard truth,
the lesson learned brutally, costing them their youth,
Anarchy is a dream, unsustainable and rare,
in practice it is, a living nightmare,

Tell the next idealist anarchist, with their eyes bright as a full moon,
anarchy isn't freedom, it is just tyranny coming soon.
Written on August 2, 2014

59
Speeding to Coruscant

The green disappears, cement and asphalt takes its place,
the process is speeding up, as if it is a race,
If this kept going, what would be the result,
if it kept going and going, without any halt,
We got a taste in star wars, the planet Coruscant,
the planet is a city, with loads of technology to flaunt,
On the surface it's great, aliens and hovercars,
with spaceships that go past light speed, and launch into the stars,
But to feed those billions, the food must be imported,
or the technology for synthetic food, was invented and supported,
From what we see there is no problem, everything flows along fine,
no one is seen starving, or waiting in line,
What we must realize, besides it being a story,
if we become Coruscant too soon, we will be sorry,
If we can't grow enough, and synthetics aren't ready,
chaos will occur, needing might to hold it steady,
So maybe all those politicians, with dollar signs in their eyes,
thinking about property taxes, from that high rise,
Should ask are we harming, our source of food,
maybe there is no problem, no need to concern or brood,
But if we are speeding to Coruscant, before the time is right,
we could sabotage our future, scarcity causes us to fight,
Remember as we develop, let's make sure it's sustainable,
or we will break down ourselves, and what will be attainable.

Written on August 3, 2014

60

Immortals

In an alternate reality, where there is less science and more magic,
is a story, heartbreaking and tragic,
Of a magic ring, that would make one a god,
just put it on, and the only way it is flawed,
For 1000 years, you will be without peers,
you will be immortal and indestructible, for all those years,
Once the time is up, the powers will slowly burn,
as the power leaves, and humanity returns,
One power hungry man, with dreams of conquest,
searched for and found the ring, so he could rule the rest,
So for over 1000 years, people lived under his fist,
with many attempts to stop him, too many to list,
Most gave up, this was just the norm,
like the sun rising, and the feeling of warm,
1180 years had passed, just another day in hell,
something was about to change, a revolutionary bell,
An MMA fighter, truly a great,
fell into the reality, through an inter-dimensional gate,
He looked around puzzled, seeing a bygone era,
when he saw a beauty, he heard her name was Farrah,
He asked where he was, she answered the Land of Mantel,
she looked strangely, why didn't he know this as well,
He soon saw the nightmare, of those who live in fear,
Mantel's reign of terror, had always been here,
The MMA fighter named Liam, saw these people without food,
saw the hopelessness, and their resigned mood,
Liam asked why Mantel's in charge, they told Liam of his power,

Liam stopped listening, after hearing this for an hour,
Liam hated bullies, he wasn't afraid of their God,
he told them to follow him, to reveal Mantell is a fraud,
As they went towards the castle, town after town followed to watch,
a spark of hope had been lit, a reason to set down their scotch,
Liam challenged Mantell, unafraid of the story,
Mantell turned to the crowd, and said this one will be gory,
Mantell told Liam, leave and he will live,
or it will be brutal, the execution he will give,
Liam stood tall, ready for the fight,
ready to die, ready to face Mantell's might,
Mantell leapt towards Liam, but was flipped to the ground,
but struck back at Liam, an enormous echoing sound,
They exchanged punches and kicks, as the crowd looked on,
seeing Mantell vulnerable, his intimidation was almost gone,
Until Liam wrestled him down, and snapped his arm in half,
as his scream echoed, leaving shock with no laughs,
Suddenly Mantell was human, as Liam raised his arms in victory,
not realizing in this reality, he had made history,
As the moment sunk in, the crowd erupted with joy,
as tears of happiness, went down the cheeks of girls and boys,
Their dreams had come true, as many had ranted,
they finally had, what we take for granted,
We had no invincible tyrants, stopping our progress and thus,
we are all human, with no immortals to rule us.
Written on August 10, 2014.

61
Economic Cheat Code

When you play a video game, you are bound,
to the rules, limits, permanently or perhaps for that round,
Some people have devices, that let you cheat the game,
you can get what you want, and continue just the same,
Except now you have an advantage, from the outside,
you have this extra tool privilege, from a free ride,
Now take a step back, away from a digital screen,
and see what lies beyond, the pixels that can be seen,
A much larger game is playing out, the game of supply and demand,
labour, goods and services, have to follow an invisible hand,
People in the western world, had a standard of living,
and the ability to demand, what salaries management was giving,
Until one day a cheat code was discovered, go to an impoverished nation,
where they have no demand, little hope of wealth creation,
It is not a coincidence, that the factories are in China today,
a country beaten down by communism, with sweatshop labour being their
way,
Other countries have corrupt governments, where people are filled with fear,
if they speak up, they will simply disappear,
If you think you're afraid to ask for a raise, imagine how afraid they are,
so how did this happen, how did it get this far,
We fought for our own freedom, and believed we lived in a bubble,
forgetting that when some are held down, it will always lead to trouble,
If everyone had rights, and could demand better wages,
this would lead to something greater, down through the ages,
Fair trade would become reality, and alliances could form,
England and France were enemies, now peace is the norm,

The next great step, is communication through the internet,
I hope people are ready for freedom, soon if not yet,
The time has finally come for us, to battle fascism, subtle or overt,
and realize that when some are oppressed, sooner or later we all get hurt.
Written on August 22, 2014.

62
Your Attention

She tells her parents she has straight A's,
hoping for a few minutes of their busy days,
will she get their attention this time,
A neglected boy pulls out all the stops,
even getting arrested by the cops,
will he have their attention because of a crime,
A teen alone and dressed in black,
with bruises on her arms and back,
does she have your attention yet,
A guy breathing fire for a crowd,
as success or injury is wondered aloud,
does he have their attention because they can bet,
A woman with cosmetic surgeries that list a mile,
with the most perfect fake smile,
does she have your attention because of her double D's,
A man stands on a ledge ready to leap,
overcome with pain ready to weep,
could he have your attention please,
Just a few examples, of those trying to be heard,
how much attention does one need, the answer is blurred,
If we extended our hands more often,
the walls of isolation would soften,
We would feel more connected less likely to lash out,
would it help those on the edge I have no doubt,
We might even prevent a hand, from pulling a trigger on others, wow,
maybe that goes too far, but do I have your attention now.
Written on August 24, 2014.

63
Songs and the Soul

With so many songs available, in the palm of your hand,
so many artists and genres, to play at your command,
Consider the following, which ones stand out,
which ones are your favourites, why have you chosen this route,
Sure the music helps, the right rhythms and beats are key,
but sometimes they speak, directly to you and me,
Sometimes they reflect our joy, confidence and what we wear,
sometimes they speak to our sorrow, our anger and despair,
When you hear a line that stands out, and repeats in your mind,
ask how it relates to you, what in you does it find,
Does it find a depression, that lurks deep inside,
does it find what separates you from people, that gap that is so wide,
To some it's meaningless fun, just dance and smile,
but some of us want more, than another distraction from the pile,
Some want answers, to what's in their heart and soul,
I wish all the best, to those trying to be whole,
I try to think about the meaning, at least a few minutes every day,
start exploring who you are, start by pressing play.
Written on August 29, 2014.

64
Stuck

Things aren't changing, I am only dreaming,
but if they don't change soon, I will start screaming,
Tired of pushing a boulder uphill, the illustration of futility,
things don't get better, regardless of my humility,
All that hard work means nothing, all that character even less,
I just want to climb up, not say I'm the best,
Stuck in the same relationships, the same problems time after time,
fighting over all sorts of things, down to every single dime,
That trapped feeling, that leaves you feeling caged,
but pretend everything is fine, your happiness must be staged,
People don't understand, maybe they were never stuck,
or they just spit out clichés, to hide that they don't give a fuck,
What can you do, is there anything at all,
how you go about this, that's your call,
If it can't be fixed, not even some day,
find what makes you miserable, create a plan to break away,
Look forward to a fresh start, take a calculated risk,
it might give you what you want, like changing the compact disc,
If you succeed, you have my congratulations,
you can inspire others, and ignite motivations,
If you don't, at least you tried,
you refused to the trapped, and showed courage bona fide,
Of course don't be reckless, look carefully at the options on the shelf,
but living a miserable life, is dangerous in itself.
Written on September 5, 2014.

65
The Walls

A man in a jail cell, stares at the cement wall,
he begins to point and laugh, so hard he nearly falls,
The others look at him, wondering what he is on,
doesn't he know where he is, is he a moron,
One day they ask him, why do you laugh at nothing,
you don't even have a TV there, at least that would be something,
He responded they take everything, from your toothbrush to your belt,
the difference between us is, I can see the walls melt,
My body may be here, but my mind can depart,
I made a decision before I arrived, I would protect my heart,
They asked him what he sees, once the walls melt,
what is it like, what has been felt,
He said he sees what was, and what will be,
once he is released, once he is free,
So as he walked away, the others left their realization unspoken,
they had let the jail win, their will had been broken,
One by one they began to laugh, at the walls that were so strong,
and had broken so many, for so, so long,
Until the guards heard the chorus, of those laughing at the walls melting away,
and one asked what was so funny, because he wanted to be as happy as they.

Written on September 12, 2014.

66
Take me away

The sun shines through the window, the melting frost is glistening,
scream up to the heavens, as if anyone is listening,
The bright future that was promised, was much duller than advertised,
assuming any of the aspirations, have been realized,
We were told that we would be stars, maybe we are clerks,
told this is all we get, it's how society works,
They call it the grind, the name is quite fitting,
how much can we take, life keeps hitting,
Finally the day comes, when we can step away,
the vacation we have waited for, tomorrow is the day,
Bags are packed, a map to another place,
as the doors close, a smile is on my face,
We will see some sights, learn a thing or two,
leave behind the old, and visit the new,
Will we see things differently, upon our return,
or return to our despair, as our spirit continues to burn,
I don't know, if everything will be okay,
all I want right now, is the car to take me away.
Written on September 19, 2014

67
The Bridge

Through the binoculars, they saw a land with riches,
how to get there, many make their pitches,
Some decide to pray, only winning over a few,
others suggested a boat, a lot of trips across the lake of blue,
Some stood up, with the knowledge and a reason to care,
help us build a bridge, so everyone can get there,
Construction began, built stone by stone,
what they would do with all that wealth, was still unknown,
As the land became closer, greed infected the owner's thoughts,
who cares about anyone else, let's take lots,
Kill two birds with one stone, save some of the cost,
take material from the start of the bridge, who cares if others are lost,
The bridge became full of holes, step on it if you dare,
a lucky or informed few, will actually make it there,
Finally the owners made it, with a lucky extra few,
leaving others sabotaged, their dreams of life anew,
Was destroyed with greed, as they watched from afar,
celebrating like kings, wealth without par,
Desperation set in, to those who were left behind,
to an island of scarcity, that was truly unkind,
The rage compounded, they had helped build that bridge to glory,
now it mocked them every day, they were the losers of the story,
They built rafts and boats, and as they arrived at the beach,
their anger was greater than reason, they would rather kill than teach,
They lit their torches, as the call of war did sound,
but what happened in the crossfire, all the riches burned to the ground,
When the dust settled, the land was a shadow of what it was,

Peter Howe

all the wealth disappeared, that is what war does,
Perhaps the generosity of a few, combined with the reason of many,
could have multiplied the riches, rather than reduce it to pennies,
Now that broken bridge, stands as the trigger of the revolution,
rather than what it could have been, the start of a better evolution.
Written on September 20, 2014

68
Mekysto's Mistake

Somewhere out there, who call themselves the fnutuss,
they are 40 foot brown orange reptiles, frightening giants to us,
They had reached a point, they were ready to explore the universe,
all they needed were crews of 5, captain, technician, co-pilots and a nurse,
The crew was in between solar systems, when ours was found by their radar,
the technician ran the calculations, and saw that it wasn't too far,
They figured out the habitable zone, and saw that earth was right in the middle,
this raised their hopes a lot, their disappointments had left them so little,
As they got closer, the other co-pilot was very tired,
he needed hibernation, just four hours and he'd emerge wired,
So the nurse and one co-pilot, left to set up hibernation,
the captain and technician went to eat, just hunger not starvation,
This left Mekysto, the screw up who hides the errors he does,
he would have never been part of the crew, if they knew how incompetent he was,
He thought he pressed the right button, give the scout camera an early start,
when the screen asked to confirm a code, an action in which he rarely took part,
He pressed confirmation, and he awaited Captain Portzoy's praise,
showing off his skills, and his ambitious ways,
Mekysto announced, as Captain Portzoy and the technician came back,
he had sent the scout camera, Portzoy asked why the screen was black,
Mekysto said the camera takes a few minutes, it hadn't been that long,
Captain Portzoy knew better, something was seriously wrong,
He went through the actions, his skin developed stress nodes,
when he turned to Mekysto, "don't you know the codes,

You dropped an Ion bomb, a million times the power of a stun gun,
you may have killed innocent beings, do you realize what you've done,"
The scout camera was sent down, to where the bomb had dropped,
most of it hit the ocean, but then Portzoy's heart almost stopped,
Several thousand humans were dead, he saw the sorrow of the others,
there were parents, children, friends, sisters and brothers,
All weeping at this loss, a truly sorrowful faction,
leaving Portzoy unsure, of the next course of action,
Should he confront them, or should they fly away,
would the humans understand, or must it wait another day,
Portzoy made a decision, it was a risky plan,
they would reveal themselves, to the world of man,
They found satellites transmitting the internet, there is no hope without
communication,
they downloaded geography and languages, to prepare for the conversation,
Is there any worse way, to introduce yourself to a planet,
because of an accident with a weapon, so dangerous some wanted to ban it,
Portzoy had Mekysto restrained, as they approached the teleportation doors,
they were going to Ottawa, because the attack was on Canada's shores,
Portzoy and Mekysto, beamed inside the parliament,
the fear of these giants was obvious, no need for a hint,
With a translation and atmosphere helmet, Portzoy's voice was heard,
as the army was notified, struggling to believe a word,
"We came looking for life, Mekysto committed a terrible error,
we never meant to cause, all this death and terror,
Our deepest condolences, goes to you and your kind,
we hope that you will forgive us, with this in mind,

Please judge Mekysto, as you would judge your own,
the Fnutuss wish to be your friends, you don't have to be alone,"
One human spoke up and asked, "how do we know you are sincere,
you're so much bigger and more powerful, surely you understand our fear,"
Mekysto spoke up, "I am being handed over to you,
from this day onward our species will start working with you"
Another human stood up and said, "even if we accept this apology of yours,
others will see this, as the beginning of many wars,"
Portzoy looked at all these humans, judging all his kind for Mekysto's crime,
it wasn't sinking in, Portzoy had one thing to say this time,
"Will you put in this much effort, to correct your mistakes as you go on living,
instead of being suspicious of us, ask why are they so unforgiving."
Written on September 21, 2014

69
Kingdom of Clouds

One day a simple criminal, another thug of the street,
was walking through the thickest fog, "I can't see a thing" said and repeat,
Suddenly it lifted him off the ground, without realizing he was being embraced,
it was bestowing him with a gift, a new power to be faced,
He could control the clouds, bring them up and down,
east, west, north, south, standing over the world a king with a crown,
He looked around at all the clouds, all this land all for him,
doing whatever he wished, anytime, at a whim,
He stole a Ferrari first, and drove around the sky,
what an incredible thrill, he was on a tremendous high,
He started taking more, he raided armoured cars and escaped,
he needed places to put his riches, clouds filled the holes that gaped,
Within a couple days, the story had spread,
was there a crook in the clouds, every idea was said,
As he pulled more clouds together, they became more dense,
which was making them harder to move, making him more tense,
He thought he was set, anything he wanted he could take,
who would go after him, he's in the clouds for pete's sake,
But now those perfect white clouds, had become a field of grey,
this is what he ignored, never thinking there would be a day,
When a rainstorm would occur, as they burst one by one,
he tried to stop them, but it couldn't be done,
His bags of money fell through, as did other stolen things,
his panic was increased, when he lost the diamond rings,
As hard as he tried, the Ferrari fell and smashed to scraps,
he screamed no remembering, all of those fun laps,

Finally his ground was running out, as he finally fell,
how did it come to this, it was all going so well,
The rain drops hit his face, as he fell faster and faster,
his kingdom had fallen apart, into a complete disaster,
Before he hit the ground, he realized it was unsustainable,
paradise is and never will be, so easily attainable,
He continued to fall, bracing for the fatal Impact,
the air left his lungs, accepting his death as fact,
As the storm quieted, people gathered to see where he landed,
his body would soon be taken away, not to be abandoned,
They weren't sure what to say, not sure what to speak aloud,
until a child said more than intended, "will anyone else fall from the clouds"
They were suddenly speechless, as they wandered through their thoughts,
but all they could say with confidence was, "I sure hope not."
Written on October 4, 2014.

70
Decisions

In the near future, genes will be accessible and change,
this could be positive, but how far will the decisions range,
Imagine preventing diabetes and heart disease, before people are born,
none of that would be missed, what a bright healthy morn,
You could prevent Osteoporosis, so they're bones will be real strong,
why stop with bones, muscles could last so long,
You could prevent dementia, cut mental illness off at the path,
while we are there make them just smart enough, so they will be good at math,
Give them skin that won't have cancer, that is a dangerous threat,
while we are at it make them good looking, so socially they will be set,
Give them great vision, we want them to always be able to see,
make their eyes a pretty blue, what a beauty they will be,
Do you now see, the double-edged sword,
here is a question, avoiding it we can't afford,
If you ever can decide everything, from personality, to profession, to height,
why did you decide everything for them, what gives you the right?
Written on October 8, 2014

71
The M Word

What started as simple agreements, you help me and I help you,
have become so much bigger, notions staggering if true,
What is morality, what is right and wrong,
the answer won't be easy, and is so, so long,
But one question goes further, haunting philosopher's minds,
is morality objective and fixed, or subjective with changing kinds,
Some say morality changes, as society evolves and grows,
leaving some to fear, if this belief is what society sows,
What could be unleashed, what suffering could unfold,
if society decides, it's new virtue is being cold,
Imagine your nightmare, one day having a green light,
there is something to fear, something to fight,
But this idea is a logistical nightmare, if it is society's call,
what is a society, a question with an ugly wall,
Is it a town, a region, a country, state or province,
there are many different practices, the thought of them all makes me wince,
So a society can't be defined, in a philosophical sense,
but it gets even uglier, more troublesome and dense,
How can we be judged, it seemed right at the time,
how can we judge others, for what we see as a crime,
If we could define a society, how can we criticize their law,
it is their view, it is what they saw,
So if we can judge other societies, far away or in the past,
then does objectively morality win, do we have the answer at last,
Not even close, excuses are made for history,
if someone owned and traded slaves today, what they would be is no mystery,
Yet Columbus is honoured, his achievement outshines his shame,

so if we don't believe in objective or subjective, what is this game,
How can we judge some harshly, and show others such lenience,
the simple answer is, today's morality is convenience,
Long ago someone gave us the rules, so we don't have to think,
but not that one, or that one, watch the consistency sink,
Some say God gave us the rules, that's how we know what is right,
but how do you know, are you bowing to the power of might,
With no explanation, just because they said so,
leaves you with no answers, no way to really know,
So now that this web, is tangled beyond belief,
and several things have been mentioned, that tend to bring grief,
What is the answer, can it ever be discovered,
if we have lost our way, can it ever be recovered,
Let's examine our criticisms, of other ways,
how others ran society, in their glory days,
We call out the irrational, the bigots and the violent,
we trash the Nazis because they were all three, and criticize those who
remained silent,
If we can judge others with reason, why can't we look in the mirror,
have an open mind, as well as an open eye and ear,
So there is objective morality, but the puzzle remains unsolved,
thousands of pieces remain unplaced, as several remain uninvolved,
But we have figured out some things, as reason became triumphant,
in those brief battles we celebrated, and played aloud the trumpet,
If we want the most moral society, let's leave no stone unturned,
we are not perfect, but we should be able to say what we've learned.
Written on October 17, 2014.

Conclusion

I hope this gave you plenty to think about, I hope that this helped give you a new way of looking at things, I don't know exactly when my next book is coming out, but I have plenty of ideas. This book may get under some people's skins, it's entirely possible that some of the ideas I expressed were wrong, but the first step to truly being enlightened is being willing to reconsider your own position. Thank you for reading, thank you for giving my ideas a chance. I look forward to entertaining and opening a conversation with you in the future.

Finally, I want to say to any young writers out there that writing is not always easy, it takes a lot of thought and a lot of contemplation as well as some knowledge of the world you live in. I hope this book inspires others to express themselves in some constructive way. If this book inspires other people greater than myself to make art, and their art in turn, inspires people who are even greater that would be a wonderful thing.

About the Author

Peter Howe was born outside of Toronto, Ontario, Canada in 1988.

He graduated from the University of Guelph-Humber with a bachelor's degree in business administration. Ultimately, he decided to branch out beyond book-keeping and accounting to incorporate more of his interests into his life. His broad knowledge and passions contribute to his desire to write and express himself in poetic ways.

Made in the USA
Charleston, SC
04 November 2015